Jim Dine: Five Themes

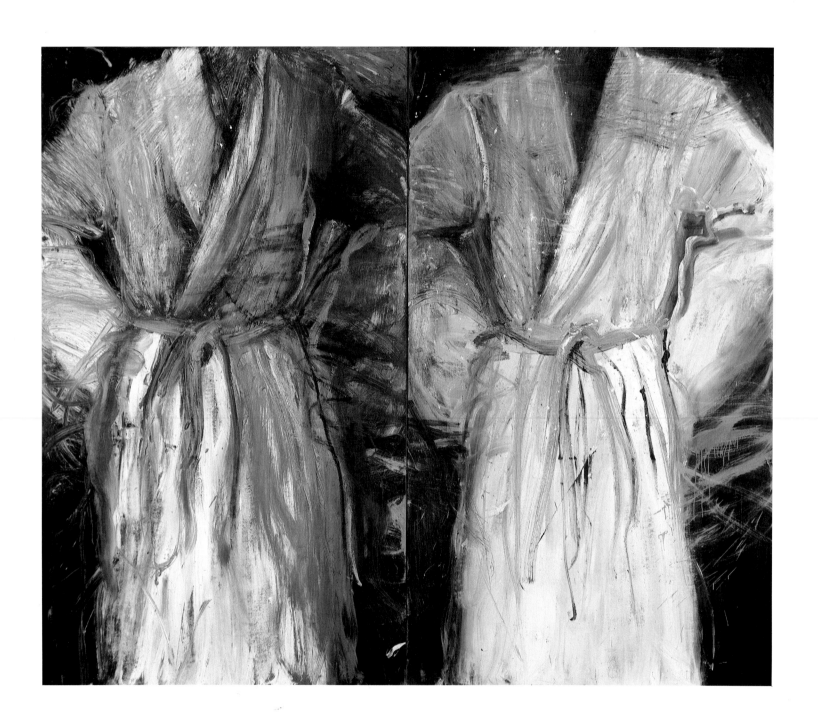

by Graham W. J. Beal

with contributions by Robert Creeley, Jim Dine
and Martin Friedman

Jim Dine: Five Themes

Walker Art Center · Minneapolis
Abbeville Press · Publishers · New York

(cover)
Painting a Fortress for the Heart
1981
acrylic on canvas
84 x 120
Collection Graham Gund

(frontispiece)
Two Mighty Robes at Night in Jerusalem   1980
oil on canvas
89½ x 106 (2 panels)
Collection Milly and Arnold Glimcher

The organization and national tour of *Jim Dine: Five Themes* have been generously supported by Best Products Co., Inc. and the National Endowment for the Arts.

The exhibition's Minneapolis presentation has been made possible by the General Mills Foundation, The McKnight Foundation and the Minnesota State Arts Board.

Library of Congress Cataloging in Publication Data

Beal, Graham William John.
    Jim Dine, five themes.

    Catalog of an exhibition held at the Walker Art Center, Minneapolis.
    Includes index.

    1. Dine, Jim, 1935–   —Exhibitions. I. Dine, Jim, 1935–   . II. Walker Art Center. III. Title.
N6537.D5A4 1984   709'.2'4
83-21467
ISBN 0-89659-414-9
ISBN 0-89659-415-7 (pbk.)

Unless otherwise indicated, works are collection the artist. Dimensions are in inches; height precedes width.

From Pop to Passion 7
Martin Friedman

Something to Hang Paint On II
Graham W. J. Beal

An appreciation by Robert Creeley precedes
illustrations of each of the five themes.

Tools 48

Robes 70

Hearts 94

Trees 118

Gates 134

For J. D. .145
Robert Creeley

Biography .150

Selected Bibliography 151

Lenders to the Exhibition 153

Index of Illustrations 156

Commentaries by Jim Dine on specific works
occur throughout the book.

From Pop to Passion

Martin Friedman

One of the most fascinating aspects of recent American art is the transformed status of those brash young painters and sculptors who made their noisy debuts in the early 1960s. Once exponents of the irreverent Pop phenomenon that challenged the primacy of high art, i.e. Abstract Expressionism, they have since become old masters themselves, remote from the crosscurrents that constitute today's art scene. Instead, they now elaborate in relative tranquility on themes and stylistic approaches they pioneered in their youth. This is true of the so-called neo-Dadaists, Jasper Johns and Robert Rauschenberg, who carried collage to the nth power in audacious "combine" paintings that incorporated chunks of the actual environment. It's the case with Roy Lichtenstein, whose imagery ennobled the comic strip, and with James Rosenquist, whose paintings apotheosized the dreams on American billboards. It's also true of Claes Oldenburg who now spends his time bringing into existence his urban monuments that were only fantasies in the 1960s: one day a giant upside-down flashlight in Las Vegas; another, a heroic umbrella on a Des Moines plaza; and on another, a colossal garden hose in Freiburg, West Germany. Even Andy Warhol, the penultimate embodiment of the free-form 60s, has become a good gray eminence. There's no escaping one's destiny.

Though somewhat younger than most of his Pop brethren, Jim Dine, too, has turned away from the flash and dazzle of that much publicized style. Over the last two decades his painting has undergone profound changes, shifting from ironic commentary on the everyday world to moody introspection.

Soon after he arrived in New York in 1958, fresh from art school in Athens, Ohio, he became active in the Pop scene which he entered with enthusiasm and wit. His conceptions were startlingly theatrical, executed with brio; they were a vibrant mélange of actual and painted objects. Fragments of the real world, embedded in and projecting from spontaneously painted canvases, they were his responses to the permissive atmosphere of Pop. In his all-embracing vision, palettes, lethal-looking axes and lawnmowers were freely juxtaposed. But even at that early stage it was evident that Dine, despite his effort to present such mundane themes with detachment, was anything but disengaged. Though working within the conventions of Pop Art he was as concerned with the act of painting as with the forms he depicted—probably more so. Perceptible beneath the cool facade of his early pictures was a restless spirit.

For all his identification with Pop Art, Dine was never a central figure in the movement and though his New York life was filled with vivid activity, including performances in his and other artists' Happenings, he was never really at ease there. Vast ambition and self-doubt are a volatile mixture. On the one hand he was developing a visible artistic identity; on the other, he was experiencing conflicts between the need to maintain the detachment that was the hallmark of Pop spirit and a constant urge to paint in a freer, more subjective fashion.

Though in the center of the 1960s New York art world, Dine regarded himself as the odd man out. "I stayed to myself, cranky and difficult to get on with sometimes," he recalls. He felt compelled to stand out in the heady melee. Instead of devoting himself fully to painting, he says, "I was immediately a performer at Happenings. My art itself was about performance." Despite the success—or notoriety—of such Dine Happenings as *Car Crash* and *The Smiling Workman* he began having emotional difficulties, vascillating between highs and lows and wanting nothing more than to escape the tumultuous art scene. In 1967, he gave up performances and New York itself when he, his wife and three children moved to London, which he had visited for the first time the year before. There, in a rented studio, Dine found the necessary seclusion to recommence painting in earnest. Productive as the London experience turned out to be, the complete expatriate existence was not for Dine and in 1971 he purchased a farm in Putney, Vermont. Now he divides his time between the two places.

Over the last decade his paintings have assumed a gravity that borders on the ominous, and though the old wryness shows itself in his unique juxtapositions of objects—tree branches that border thickly brushed canvas surfaces and great blue clamps adhered to painted hearts—his art has become more intuitive and self-revelatory. His symbols have taken on a frenzied existence of their own as they materialize through fierce and reckless paint strokes. This transformation of Dine from popster to turbulent expressionist is not surprising; he has always been less interested in social commentary than the mystique of painting. For him the object has always been the touchstone to visionary possibilities. He talked about such things even in his extroverted Pop days and in a 1963 *Art News* interview with G. R. Swenson, declared:

> *I'm interested in personal images, in making paintings about my studio . . . I'm working on a series of palettes right now, I put down the palette first, then within that palette I can do anything—clouds can roll through it, people can walk over it, I can put a hammer in the middle of it. Every time I do something, the whole thing becomes richer; it is another thing added to the landscape.*

For Dine, then, objects were means to greater ends and like his fellow popsters he focused intensely on a few symbols from his immediate environment. Over the course of many paintings, these took on deeper meaning, reflecting shifts in his emotional state. Sometimes they even fused. The five themes included here—Tools, Robes, Hearts, Trees and Gates—are cryptic symbols that can convey a wide range of mood—from airy and buoyant to heavy and morose.

The Trees and Gates are the least specific in form of the five themes. They emerge, as it were, from a mystical haze and, as Dine suggests, have willed themselves into existence. This is particularly true of the trees whose spectral shapes writhe across the canvas. These torso-like forms, whose limbs suggest outstretched arms, are violently scrawled improvisations on the contours of Dine's earlier Robe paintings, images that he acknowledges are self-portraits. The elegiac trees, composed of heavy skeins of dark pigment, are at the opposite end of the emotional spectrum from Dine's recent Gate series. In Dine's commentaries that accompany the illustrations of his works, he reflects on his long-valued association with Aldo Crommelynck, the eminent French master printer in whose atelier he has made numerous etchings over the last ten years. Dine's desire to commemorate their friendship led to the Gate theme. The motif derives from the curvilinear forms of the great 19th-century wrought iron gate before the Crommelynck atelier. So taken was he with it, that several large paintings, a mass of drawings and a monumental sculpture have followed.

The full significance of Dine's themes remains elusive, even to him. Their meaning as conveyors of emotion far outweighs their descriptive qualities, but ultimately, he says, they refer to the act of artistic invention: "I've tried to make paintings that are about painting."

Something to Hang Paint On

Graham W. J. Beal

I always have to find some theme, some tangible subject matter besides the paint itself. Otherwise I would have been an abstract artist. There are times when I would have loved to have been one, I mean a nonobjective artist, so-called, but I always have to find something to hang the paint on. I have tried painting without objects, painting without subject matter except the paint. It comes to nothing because it is nothing. It doesn't interest me. I'm not a minimal person, hardly an abstract person. I need that hook . . . something to hang my landscape on. Something.

Jim Dine's work is characterized by the emergence, disappearance, and reemergence of a handful of motifs. Tools, Robes and Hearts have dominated his output for more than twenty years. Dine's long, complex transition from Pop assemblagist to painterly expressionist has caused various dramatic transformations in that time, always nurtured by his personal and artistic development and his response to trends in the art world. There have been expeditions into other territories—most notably the hallucinatory still-life paintings of the late 1970s, which bear little or no relationship to the greater part of Dine's output—but only since 1980 has the tyranny of the three themes been effectively challenged by iconographic newcomers, the Gates and Trees.

Note: Most of Jim Dine's comments are from a series of interviews with the author taped in the artist's Los Angeles studio in February 1982 and in his London studio in October 1982. The others are from a videotaped talk with Martin Friedman of November 1981.

Their form and treatment, far removed from the work of the 1960s, confirm his emergence as a full-blooded expressionist in the postwar American tradition.

A precocious talent some ten years younger than the artists usually considered to be his peers, Dine was still in his mid-twenties when he became a leading figure in the artistic explosion that followed the maturity of Abstract Expressionism. His career began in the New York of the late 1950s and very early 1960s, the heyday of the Happening. A heady combination of performance, painting and sculpture, the Happening was an attempt to demolish all barriers separating art and life. Unlike other masters of the Happening such as Allan Kaprow and Claes Oldenburg who, through scripts and diagrams, exercised considerable control over the course of each event, Dine tended to use his Happenings as a form of catharsis, reenacting in them dramatic moments from his own life. Even Dine's elaborate *Car Crash* of 1960 was based on a real accident involving the artist and his wife. This turbulent confluence of art and life was startlingly expressed in another 1960 piece, *The Smiling Workman,* a thirty-second virtuoso performance featuring Dine gulping down cans of actual paint as he scrawled the words "I love what I'm doing" on a nearby scenery flat.

For all its brevity and youthful joie de vivre, *The Smiling Workman* vividly highlights the two poles of Dine's creative process. On the one hand the furious expressionistic energy and the total association of himself with the artistic act; on the other, the acknowledgment of the existence of the everyday world, embodied here in the mundane words "smiling," "workman," "doing." No such polarity existed in the minds of the abstract expressionists. For them the creative act was supreme. All references to the outside world were banished and the artist thereby freed to create purely abstract images that mirrored his subconscious. As early as the mid-1950s, Jasper Johns and Robert Rauschenberg defused this highly charged gestural style by incorporating it within the framework of recognizable imagery or everyday artifacts. In Johns's work of 1953 it is the American flag that serves as a sort of straitjacket for the expressionistic surface of the image. Rauschenberg revitalized the collage technique by combining photographs, drawings and fabrics with abstract expressionisticlike brushwork.

Dine soon came to feel that his Happenings were too personal, that there was not enough perspective between art and life. Consequently, his assemblage paintings of the early 1960s are in stark contrast to the emotive Happenings that immediately preceded them. Ironic and imbued with skepticism, his work after 1962 clearly reflects a change of tempo. His loose brushwork descends from the abstract expressionists, but his persistent inclusion of common objects asserts his independence from them. Dine likens this relationship to that between a father and his son, and throughout

*Double Isometric Self-Portrait
(Serape)* 1964
oil on canvas with objects
56⅞ x 84½
Collection Whitney Museum of
American Art
Gift of Helen W. Benjamin in
memory of her husband, Robert
M. Benjamin

the 1960s his work was very much a testimony to the independence of the son. Such works as *Five Feet of Colorful Tools* (p 13) or *Double Isometric Self-Portrait (Serape)* (p 15) are characterized by a distinct sense of whimsy, with tools and other objects added to undercut the sense of "high art." In fact, the use of the tools simply expresses Dine's totally inclusive attitude toward materials. For him there is little or no separation between the "real" world and the "art" world when it comes to choosing his sources.

These devices and the attitudes that underlay them inevitably recall those of the European Dada artists who, some forty years earlier, had mounted their own attack on established values. In their case the target was Cubism and the society that spawned it. Rauschenberg and Johns had no such socio-political ambitions, but the similarity of their methods to those of Marcel Duchamp and Man Ray was obvious, and for a short while they were called neo-Dadaists.

By the beginning of the 1960s, however, Rauschenberg's idiosyncratic multiplicity and Johns's fastidious intellectualism had paved the way for something rather different: Pop Art. In an extended annus mirabilis, between 1962 and 1964, a bewildering variety of artistic talents found their careers launched under the gaudy Pop banner. For those whose work employed imagery drawn from popular culture, or whose methods mimicked the mechanics of mass production, the term Pop, in itself, was not a bad one, but many artists

discovered that the real nature and subject matter of their work was obscured by this occasionally useful label.

The tendency of some Pop artists to annex bits and pieces of the outside world as their subject matter was not for Dine, whose themes, or subject matter, have always been intensely personal. "The coat hangers are Jasper's," he says. "I choose what's familiar to me. I would never choose a coat hanger; it has nothing to do with *me*." This is far removed from the detachment of other artists of his generation, seen in extreme form in Andy Warhol's arbitrary, almost random method of selecting motifs. Dine's sense of possession has to be complete: "I used to say that the bathrobe looked like I was in it. Not anymore. Now I feel it's such a familiar thing that I own it."

Such singular identification was lacking in some early Dine themes and they quickly faded from view. The bathroom, the necktie and the artist's palette were all leitmotifs between 1961 and 1964 but have not reappeared since. The necktie, early evidence of Dine's continuing interest in the relationship between personality and clothing, which was to find mature expression in the robe images, was a regular feature of the 1961 paintings but only subsequently appeared in the graphic work. Dine attaches no particular significance to this and feels that it could appear again at any time, just as Hearts and Robes have been recycled. The tie, in fact, gave way to jackets and trousers that, in turn, soon gave way to robes. For a

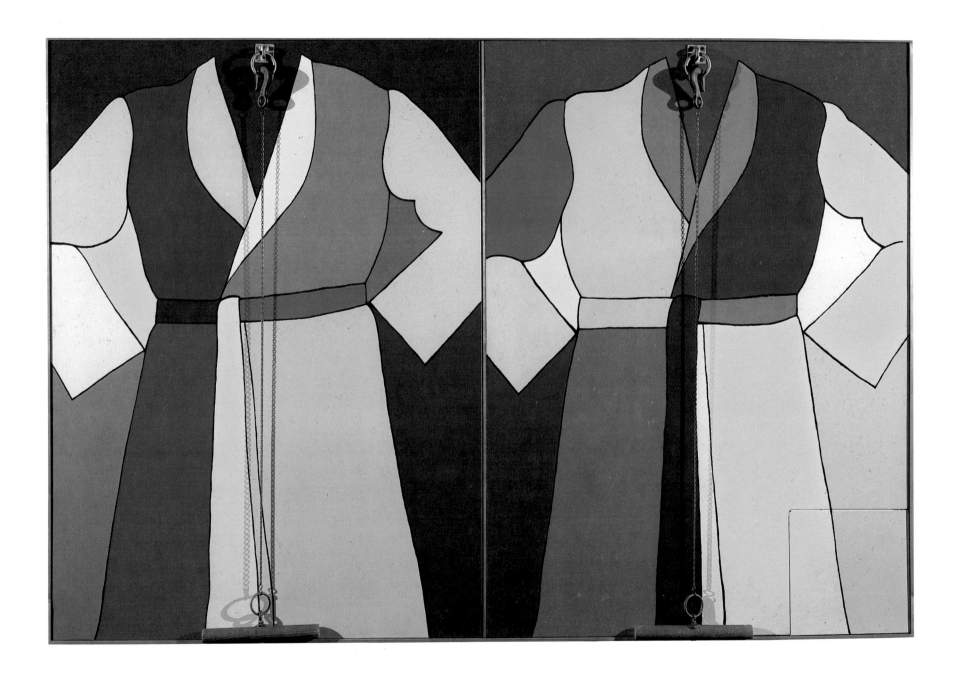

Marcel Duchamp
In Advance of the Broken Arm
1915
wood and metal "ready made"
snow shovel
47¾ high
Collection Yale University
Art Gallery
Gift of Katherine S. Dreier for
the Collection Société Anonyme

Lawnmower 1962
oil on canvas with object
77½ x 36
Collection Mrs. Florence Teiger

*I painted the Lawnmower in East
Hampton, Long Island, in the
summer of 1962. It was the first time
our family had ever taken a holiday.
We had two little kids then, and we
rented the house of a painter. I had
had a show the winter before at the
Martha Jackson Gallery of ties and
other objects, and we had a little
money for a change. I was almost
sexually stimulated by going into the
hardware stores out there, and it was
the first time I could afford to buy
the tools I wanted, to use as paint or
next to paint. I just put the
lawnmower there, and it was right,
and painting those references to the
landscape was a big thrill, like
hitting a home run. And, of course,
I got the usual comments, "You
know, it's not really art, you're
crazy," etcetera.*

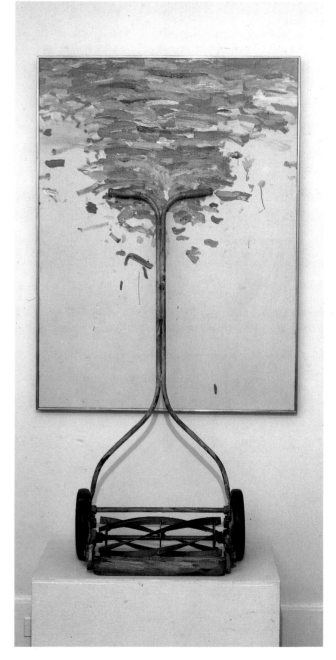

Flesh Bathroom with Yellow Light and Objects 1962
oil on canvas; mixed media
70½ x 61 x 7
Collection The St. Louis Art Museum; purchase
funds given by the Shoenberg Foundation, Inc.

short while, however, it indeed looked as if Dine was the "owner" of the tie.

On the other hand, very much a shared property around 1962 was the "bathroom" theme. Not since Degas and Bonnard has this private realm been so minutely scrutinized. David Hockney, Roy Lichtenstein, Claes Oldenburg, George Segal and Tom Wesselmann treated a bemused public to a stream of images all featuring an assortment of naked bodies, showers, bathtubs and other porcelain furnishings. Dine confronted his feelings about the "real" and "art" worlds in the 1962 painting *Flesh Bathroom with Yellow Light and Objects*. Four bathroom accoutrements mounted on a delicately modulated painted canvas convert a self-contained, spiritually elevated, abstract expressionist painting into a partial representation of a room associated with distinctly unelevated activities. Unlike Wesselmann, whose pristine bathrooms are always inhabited by equally pristine nudes, Dine chose not to depict a figure. Instead, the first word of the title, that ostensibly describes the pinkish hues of the painted canvas, also unequivocally introduces the idea of human presence and at the same time emphasizes the physicality of the painted surface. Further, the real world is actually reflected in the mirrored cabinet, literally incorporating the viewer into the painting. This is, perhaps, Dine's tongue-in-cheek reference to the abstract expressionist concept that their paintings are arenas within which they perform, and into which the responsive spectator is inevitably drawn.

Dine continued this line of investigation in another audacious crossbreed work, the 1962 *Lawnmower* (p 16), an ironic concoction of equal parts found object and unique painting. *Lawnmower* invites comparison with Marcel Duchamp's ready-made sculpture of 1915, a snow shovel tantalizingly titled *In Advance of the Broken Arm* (p 16). Dine's garden machine, however, is not an unadorned objet trouvé, baldly challenging the viewer to dispute its validity as a work of art. The lawnmower itself rests against the canvas and the upper part is liberally daubed with gestural brushmarks—a sort of double homage to Monet and Pollock—that extend onto the handle of the mower and down to the blades and roller. On the one hand, the lawnmower seems to literally sweep out of the canvas, its relationship to the painting and its value as an art object confirmed by its oil paint-daubed frame. On the other hand, leaning against the canvas, the lawnmower's mundane reality seems to rebuke the limitations of painting.

Although Dine kept a distance from the Pop Art furor, by 1962 he had established something of a reputation and a small measure of financial independence that had enabled him to give up teaching in the previous year and concentrate on his work. "It was," he says, "an unusual summer. I didn't leave the house apart from when I walked to my studio and back. I could do that, but otherwise . . . I couldn't leave the house. That summer I really painted like crazy."

Tools

Among the "paintings" created in the summer of 1962 was *Black Garden Tools* (p 21). It is difficult to imagine anything less Pop Art-like than this implacable image. Its true kinsmen are the Jasper Johns paintings of 1961–64 which feature attached or hanging household objects, kitchen utensils, paint rollers, brushes, rags and small hinged canvases.

Dine and Johns saw one another often in 1962. "My work shows it, obviously," Dine says, "and his does too . . . compare my *Black Garden Tools* to his *Fool's House*" (p 20). The comparison is indeed instructive but, although there are similarities, the differences are even more telling. In *Fool's House* a broom hangs on a vertically elongated canvas. A towel, a stretcher and a cup are identified in hasty handwriting along the bottom. Across the top are the words "Fool's House" dislocated to read "USE . . . FOOL'S HO." To read the title correctly the flat canvas would have to be bent into a cylinder. Although the paintings of these years are sometimes difficult to interpret, in *Fool's House* Johns gives unmistakable clues to his dilemma: he feels trapped, painting in circles, swinging mindlessly away like the inelegant broom that threatens to obliterate the brushwork. If Johns's implements unnerve the viewer, Dine's garden tools seem downright dangerous and threatening. Bludgeonlike spades, spiky rakes and forks hang like so many medieval weapons against a forbidding wall of black paint through which an underlying

membrane of color is fleetingly discerned. The innocuous garden shed has been transformed into a nightmarish dungeon. Although it is, the artist says, "rather colorful in a way," the overwhelming effect is far from lighthearted and hints at a spiritual desperation far beyond that of Johns's conceptual impasse. Dine's probe of both formal and psychological boundaries is, in short, deeply expressionistic. The tools, smeared with oily black paint, do not so much symbolize the artist's state of mind as embody it. His selection and treatment of the tools make them as personally and emotionally charged as any expressionistic brushmark.

Black Garden Tools is among a number of works combining paint and assemblage that Dine made in this 1962 summer of plenty. Several of them have an altogether brighter aspect than the unsettling black image. In *Five Feet of Colorful Tools*, a positively ebullient work, objects are suspended in front of a board which is attached to the top of the canvas. The lower three-quarters of the canvas is raw, unblemished but for a few paint splatters. The board and the top section of the canvas are, by contrast, a cacophony of color. Each of the tools was spray-painted in bright enamellike colors, leaving ghostlike images on the canvas and board background. Finally, Dine rearranged the real tools so that they hang in a new relationship to the illusions of themselves.

The overall impression of the band of tools is one of almost futuristic movement—they seem to jostle one another in a mechanistic dance, their vitality highlighted by their vibrant colors donned, as it were, for the occasion.

Dine's cheerful use of hand tools in *Five Feet of Colorful Tools* is palpable evidence of his long-standing love for these utilitarian implements, strangely shaped according to their special function and often in bright, shiny colors. Even as a youngster they stimulated his imagination and later played a dual, paradoxical role as both beautiful object and disruptive "Dada" element.

Tools occupy a special place among Dine's themes. Not only are they literally physical presences in the so-called tool paintings, they crop us as accents in paintings based on other themes. The saw in *Poulenc* (p 103) is a chunk of reality, a sharp contrast to the symbol of romantic love. In this juxtaposition of object and painting Dine draws attention to the two dominant aspects of his life: the saw is a symbol of his reality as a contemporary American; the painted canvas and the word "Poulenc" represent his sense of belonging to the Western artistic tradition.

The relationship of tool to heart is significantly different in *Blue Clamp* (p 109), a 1981 Heart painting with a heavily built-up surface. In *Poulenc* Dine consciously used the sizable saw for its menacing attitude, wanting, he says, "to make a slightly dangerous painting." In *Blue Clamp* the small device plays a purely formal role.

Between 1963 and 1970 tools appeared only sporadically in Dine's work and, with few exceptions, are minor accessories in large, austere compositions. They feature in a series of Heart paintings made in the summer and winter of 1971–72, and then, in 1973, again became the focus of his work for the next several years. Dine now began to add his favorite working implements to the earlier list: wrenches, knives, brushes, screwdrivers and scissors became the subjects of an extensive series of drawings and collages. In sharp contrast to a hitherto open-ended attitude toward the medium and materials, there appeared, virtually exclusively, a single compositional format of tools as vertical forms horizontally aligned against an overall field of canvas or paper. From work to work the only variation is the actual position of the row. It was basically the same approach employed in the 1962 tool pieces but now, ten years later, Dine used it as a device to introduce aspects of landscapes and architecture into his work.

At the very beginning of this second fruitful Tool period Dine effectively laid out the full range of ideas and forms that he was to investigate for the next few years. In the 1972 painting *Our Life Here* (p 23), the objects are scruffy little forms that contrast insistently with the atmospheric painted canvas. The numbers hint at some imaginary list that would explain the interrelationship of these disparate utensils. As the title suggests, the painting is about

Jasper Johns
Fool's House   1962
oil on canvas with objects
72 x 36
Collection Jean
Christophe Castelli

Black Garden Tools 1962
oil on wood panel with objects
60 x 60
Collection Estate of
Myron Orlofsky

Like the Lawnmower *I did this
painting in the summer of 1962. It
was bought by my best friend, Myron
Orlofsky. I used a kind of thick,
ugly, black paint that didn't have
the consistency of fancy tube oils.
The painting itself looks rather
rough and tough, and I purposely
painted bright colors underneath to
let just a little bit of them come
through.*

Our Life Here 1972
oil on canvas with objects
60 x 96

The title refers to Vermont. I used the intimate stuff picked up from my studio floor, old brushes and odd objects, and I kept painting over the ground; half of it is not actually even paint, I think it is tar.

Our Life Here is a list, a good example of my source material from childhood, like the groups of tools hung up in our store. Today, when I travel to big cities I like to go to a department store to get a feeling about the people and their relationships to objects. In the Bon Marché in Paris I spend a lot of time in the yarn and sewing department looking at the buttons and thread lined up like color charts. In New York I go to Brooks Brothers to look at the suits hanging on the racks to see how the colors go together. That little interest of mine relates to this painting in that real objects can be lined up even without an artist's use of color.

Dine's daily routine. Not only the objects but much of the pigment itself was picked up from the floor of his Vermont studio.

Beyond the real references to Dine's artistic and domestic environment, *Our Life Here* contains specific allusions to landscape painting. The swirling golden-brown hues recall the romantic landscapes of J.M.W. Turner. There is a green patch in the very center of the canvas as if the obscuring fog has, for a moment, partially lifted to give a clearer view of the land over which the tools hover like strange apparitions. Abstract painting, sculpture, landscape, surreal encounter: it is a virtual catalogue of Dine's artistic concerns.

The title of the 1973 Tool piece, *The Art of Painting No. 2* (p 57), refers to the explosive way in which this five-panel work was created. The forms are explicitly those of landscape. Furiously brushed green, brown and yellow paint evokes rich green meadows rippling under limitless cerulean skies. On each panel two tools, placed exactly on the horizontal axis, hang from proverbial skyhooks. Dine added wire extensions to several of the variously sized and proportioned objects so that they all occupy the same fourteen-inch band of space across the canvas and stand, as it were, on tiptoe above the greenery. What may seem to be a random assortment of tools is, in fact, the result of a lengthy trial-and-error process. Dine works intuitively and says of such works, "It was just a case of the right objects falling into place . . . I move them around a lot and the decisions are not based on anything conscious."

Thus, the red-tipped bristles of a broad housepainter's brush rest lightly against the green "grass" creating a standard simultaneous color contrast. Similarly, the warm orange wood of the ruler and the tool handles contrast with the elegant, cool blue of the sky.

Actual objects, mainly brushes and pencils, appear in many of Dine's Tool drawings of this period but always in subordinate roles. This was a crucial crossroad in his career, when he determined to realign some of his artistic priorities. He embarked on a self-imposed apprenticeship, forcing himself, through drawing, to address the tools directly instead of as foils to an abstract, painted field. The result is a wealth of poetic graphic images in which tools are given distinct personalities and they physically dominate the romantic drawings in a manner not previously seen in his work.

Most of the drawings are untitled, with an occasional laconic addition such as *Pliers* (from *Untitled Tool Series*) (p 61) of 1973, in distinct contrast to the overtly poetic titles of Dine's paintings. Titles have always been important to him; in the surrealist tradition, he regards them as an active component of a work that must be reconciled in the viewer's mind with the painted image. Further, the titles introduce a distinct element of time, as in *I'm Painting with My Animals* (p 99) that underlines Dine's description of himself as "a combination of

23

24

literary connotations and formalism," which has evolved from long friendships with the poets Robert Creeley and John Ashberry. At one time Dine even made a great effort to write, and published two books of poetry which he now terms "not very good, but not without interest, because the poetry is painter's poetry."

In the 1973 Tool drawings Dine focuses attention on the objects and the act of drawing them by deliberately using non-allusive titles. Even when he is being his "messy, expressionistic self," by partly obliterating carefully delineated objects with an eraser or heavy charcoal, the tools are rendered with trompe l'oeil accuracy. Even so, this is no mere hyper-realist exercise. Arranged in a row, as usual, they do not appear to lie on a flat surface but, improbably, to stand up. In a number of the drawings there is a faint horizontal line below the tools, but even where this is absent the allusion to landscape is unmistakable and the humble implements take on attributes of architecture. The point is emphasized in one untitled collage that includes a postcard of the Washington Monument. In such company the scale of the drawn tools undergoes a dramatic transformation: the scissors are a perverse version of Saarinen's monumental arch in St. Louis and the ratchet screwdriver a surreal gloss on the Sears Tower in Chicago. However, the battered work glove close to the screwdriver on the extreme right of the composition is a floppy form that defies architectural transmogrification and, at the same time, reasserts human scale. Dine has concocted a visual seesaw—the human attributes at one end, the architectural connotations at the other. The tools between are radically transfigured as the viewer's eye travels to and fro across the composition.

Dine's transformations of tools into monuments may be fleeting, but they invite comparison with the work of Claes Oldenburg who has proposed such unlikely metamorphoses of everyday objects as the clothespin as a skyscraper and the baseball bat as a monument. The latter was actually carried out, and even when Oldenburg is at his most facetious his ideas are invariably technically feasible, worked out in detail from the early fanciful sketches into drawings that are, in effect, engineer's blueprints.

In contrast to such thoroughgoing monumentality, Dine's references to architectural forms are elusive as well as allusive and the consequence, not of a relentless, if perverse logic, but of unexpected juxtapositions. The resulting ambiguity tends to be disconcerting rather than disarming, alarming rather than ironic. Dine's strong response to the colors and forms of individual tools reveals their ultimate use as vehicles for psychological expression. Their moods range from the festive air of the 1975 pastel *Shears* (p 26), that features a flamingolike pair of pruning shears set in a sparkling landscape, to the murky Doré-like habitat of the cutters in the 1974 *Untitled (Red Clippers)* (p 27).

25

Shears 1975
pastel and spray enamel on paper
with object
60½ x 38
Collection Mrs. Julius E. Davis

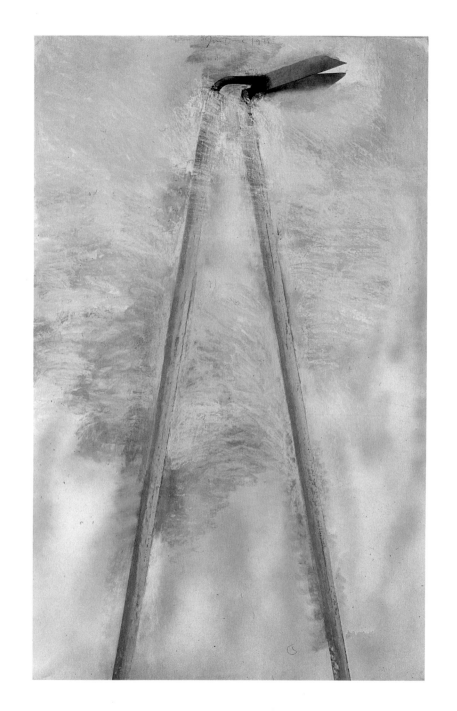

Untitled (Red Clippers) 1974
charcoal and pastel on paper
35¹⁄₁₆ x 42
Collection Hirshhorn Museum
and Sculpture Garden,
Smithsonian Institution

27

Robes

By 1975 the tool motif had almost completely faded from Dine's work. Implements sometimes appeared in large paintings, but more as incidents than foils—points of detail to draw attention to the paint surface. As Dine's confidence in his drawing ability increased, so the tools, themselves metaphors for the human form, gave way to direct depictions of the body. Dine was returning to a theme that, except in prints, he had not explored since 1964: the bathrobe.

The Robe theme emerged from a series of early 1960s paintings based on his own palette. Initially treated in much the same way as the rakes and spades of *Black Garden Tools*, the palette soon took on a life of its own, and from 1963 and 1964 there are a number of works in which its oblong silhouette is virtually the whole field of the canvas; artistic tool, artistic activity and artistic creation combined. In the earlier works, through the handling of the paint or the imagery imposed on the palette field, Dine makes references to other artists, mainly the Dadaists, especially Picabia. Before long, however, an underlying metamorphic self-portraiture invades the surface, dispelling the thin film of camaraderie.

In the stark, three-panel *3 Palettes (3 Self-Portrait Studies)* (p 29) of 1964, the partial outline of a bathrobe appears in the middle of each palette. Footprints—Dine's own—mark where he stamped his paint-laden shoes close to the right shoulder of each robe. *3 Palettes* is an uncharacteristically stringent work when compared to other palette-robe painting of this period. In *Palette (Self-Portrait No. 1)* (p 30) of 1964, a jaunty red robe dances on the black palette. The bicycle chain and wires that stretch to the canvas's lower edge are the umbilical cords that link the artist with his art.

In another 1964 painting, *Self-Portrait Next to a Colored Window* (p 31), Dine displays, in virtuoso fashion, his prodigious skills as draftsman, colorist and collage-maker. A real window frame abuts a stretched canvas on which is drawn an identical window. By painting the glass of the real window with bright, opaque colors, Dine created another complex, hybrid work: part abstract painting, part color chart, part realist image. But if nothing can be seen through the "real" window, there is, in exquisite detail, a full bathrobe visible through the illusionistic one. This bold juxtaposition of illusion and abstraction was inspired by the color charts found in hardware stores rather than from the work of hard-edge abstractionists. Color charts delight Dine not only as objects in themselves but also as hints of "what all the possibilities are." Accordingly, several panes in the illusionistic window are more heavily worked than others and correspond tonally with their exact counterparts on the painted window. The effect links the ghostly gray figure on one side with the wealth of life-imbuing colors on the other.

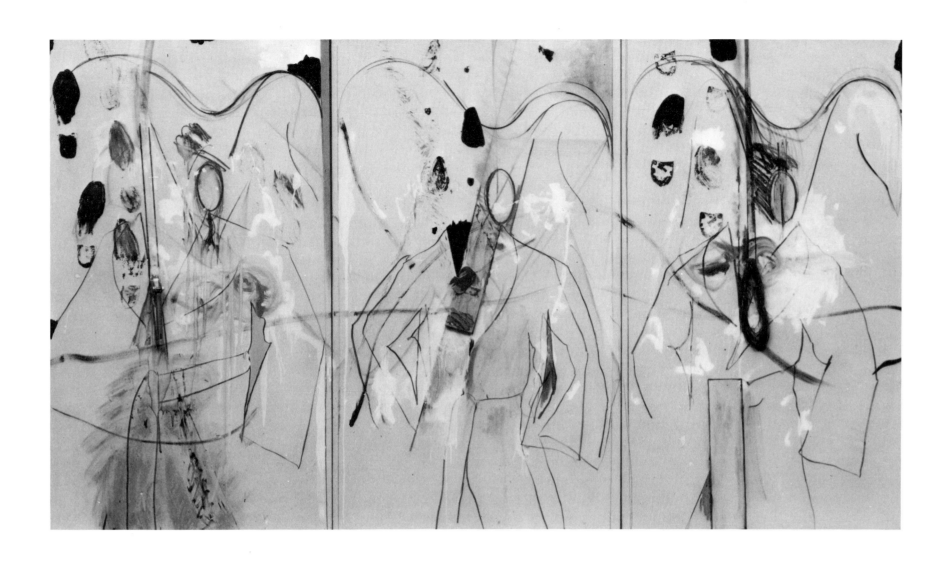

Palette (Self-Portrait No. 1)
1964
oil and collage on canvas
84½ x 60
Collection Newport Harbor
Art Museum
Gift of Mr. and Mrs. Gene
Summers

*Self-Portrait Next to a Colored
Window*   1964
charcoal on canvas, oil on glass
and wood
71⅞ x 99½ (2 panels)
Collection Dallas Museum of
Fine Arts, Dallas Art Association
purchase, Contemporary Arts
Council Fund

This painting and Charcoal Self-
Portrait in a Cement Garden *were
both made in the summer of 1964,
and here again I was involved with
color charts. As a boy my cultural
life did not necessarily come from
paintings and books but from hardware and paint stores. There I found
romance and beauty in objects.*

In a logical next step the artist explored some further "possibilities" of color. *Double Isometric Self-Portrait (Serape)* presents, again side by side, two almost identical robes. The long chains with wooden handles hanging from the necks of the figures are the isometrics, the regimen that stretches the artist to make him a fitter being. With the exception of a related single-panel version made the same year, *Double Isometric* is unique in that its clear-cut forms and cheerful color markedly separate it from the other more heavily worked images of this period. All of the 1964 bathrobes were made for an exhibition at the Sidney Janis Gallery in New York. Dine prefers to work on groups of paintings with a specific showing in mind, because, he says, he is fond of "simple-minded tasks."

Over ten years later, for a show at The Pace Gallery in New York, he once again turned to the bathrobe theme. But there had been many changes in the artist's working methods in the interim, notably the self-imposed apprenticeship in drawing that culminated, in 1975, in the figure drawings. These were the means by which Dine returned to the Robe. Although he was quite content to continue working on the figures solely through the drawing medium, he saw the Robe as a related image through which he could exploit his newly-refined skills in paint.

These new powers are clearly evident in his 1976 *Cardinal* (p 81), a brilliant, delicately modulated, red robe that glows with an almost hallucinatory intensity against a dark, velvety background. As in all the Robe paintings of this series there are no found objects to distract attention from the painted surface. If there is any relationship to the style of other artists of the period it is to such color-field mystics as Mark Rothko and Barnett Newman. The title, an allusion to the ecclesiastical princes of the Italian Renaissance and the painters such as Raphael and Titian they so lavishly patronized, puts even further distance between Dine and his Dada-related past.

Contrasting with the subtle resolution of *Cardinal* is the calculated hesitation of *Afternoon Robe* (p 33), in which an aggressive pentimento dominates the murky colors. Form and color nowhere quite coincide. The lower part of the robe is a warm red, reminiscent of *Cardinal*, but the upper section shudders under the weight of heavy, repeated strokes, an eloquent testimony to Dine's decision to make a painting about "corrections." Although there may not be two artists more temperamentally dissimilar than Matisse and Giacometti, it was their work Dine had in mind as he made *Afternoon Robe*: the obvious pleasure in the image is tempered by ubiquitous disquiet. The robe shifts in and out and from side to side, an image of a continuing existential doubt.

*The Night Forces Painterliness to
Show Itself in a Clearer Way*
1978
oil on canvas
96 x 96
Collection Mr. and Mrs.
Morton L. Janklow

Most of Dine's work at this time avoided such formal and psychological ambiguity in favor of the lyrical, contemplative intensity represented by *Four Robes Existing in This Vale of Tears* (p 78). Each robe is delicately painted and meticulously executed in dappled, pastel-like colors, and set against a dark, smoky background. The self-restraint is almost palpable. While the work undoubtedly owes much of its character to the recent drawing exercises, it has a unity and a uniformity not seen since the *Double Isometric Self-Portrait (Serape)* of 1964. Beyond this, however, there are few similarities. The earlier image, with its hard-edged coats of many colors, seems downright brash when compared to the softly-modeled robes of 1976. Instead of the implied isometrics, the artist now suggests a contemplative self-existence. The title is as subtle as Dine's new-found technique. Each word is carefully weighed: the melancholy "vale of tears" balances the quiet yet positive assertion of "existing."

In 1977 Dine quite surprisingly produced a series of still lifes that in every way but their large scale recall de Chirico, Morandi and Magritte. Bottles, teapots, seashells, skulls and vegetables march across the canvases in incongruous arrays. All are carefully delineated, but not so carefully that the sense of paint is sacrificed to straightforward realism. The objects in these still lifes, like those in Magritte's disquieting, surrealistic images, are rendered with a perplexing impartiality. The titles range from the purely melancholic *My*

Studio #1: The Vagaries of Painting "These Are Sadder Pictures" to the reluctantly optimistic *The Night Forces Painterliness to Show Itself in a Clearer Way* (p 34). Whatever impulses lay behind the creation of these images—and Dine says that he doesn't fully understand them himself—it is tempting to think, in the light of his subsequent artistic development, that the "clearer way" to painterliness was toward a freer gestural expressionism.

An early example of this tendency is *Jerusalem Nights* (p 91) of 1979. The image emerges as if spontaneously generated from the welter of brushmarks and demonstrates the degree to which Dine indeed "owns" the Robe. There is little evidence of the artist's difficulty in making such a large work in the small room he used as a studio in Israel, except that one of the two canvases juts out farther than its partner. Dine likes the idea that half the painting seems to advance, implying motion even as it suggests disjunction. A number of the earlier Robes are vertically bisected in one way or another, but the garment in *Jerusalem Nights* is unique in its actual physical cleavage.

One of the few Robe paintings bisected horizontally is *Balcony* (p 85), a 1979 oil. It was inspired by Manet's 1869 painting of the same title in which a green metal fence runs across the lower half of the canvas. A few years earlier Dine would probably have attached a real balcony simultaneously separating and uniting the painted and the real worlds in true

This was part of a larger work of sculpture done in 1967, the year I taught at Cornell. I had worked with the image around 1965 when I designed A Midsummer Night's Dream *for the Actor's Workshop of San Francisco. There it was a big decoration, an object in a forest of people, but it became an element in my work, like a hand and other familiar "everyday" images.*

I am not necessarily a "pop" artist, popular in the kitsch or the Pop Art sense, but it was in the air and one did use, for a time, primary objects, and certainly a heart is in that category. It is a lot of things, a living heart, a valentine. As a kid I liked Valentine's Day, not because I was in love, necessarily, but because I liked the redness of it. It's everything, really, a vagina, an ass; it's pretty basic stuff, this cleaved, full object.

Someone once asked me if I was referring to The Wizard of Oz *when I made the* Straw Heart. *I don't usually think that way, but it's not a bad idea. Frankly I liked the idea of it being straw, not flesh. It has an impermanent look. On the other hand, it is made of sheet iron.*

When I first used the heart I didn't know it would become an abiding theme. Typically, though, I always go where my romance takes me, so it is an emblem that I return to with a lot of affection.

assemblagist fashion. But instead of separating one kind of space from another, the sketchy painted forms of the balcony converge with those of the robe, and in some areas actually appear to be embedded in it. Although the forms are compressed the robe is still strikingly volumetric; "modernist" flatness is forcibly wedded to a modified form of illusionism. Dine's balcony is not simply a glib reference to an important picture in the history of Impressionism: it is a painting about painting. Dine has again found a way to explore the paradox between the real and the abstract.

There is a double paradox in *Light Comes upon the Old City* (p 82). Despite the Robe image, the subject is landscape; the title makes that clear. The other paradox is that although the canvas is rendered almost entirely in blacks and dark browns, the painting is also about light. This is the blinding noonday light of Jerusalem that obliterates all details and creates shadows of impenetrable darkness. The Robe, ever a flexible vehicle for Dine, is used in this case to compress time and place into a single image.

The near Pavlovian relationship in Dine's mind between the image of the Robe and the act of painting is made quite clear by the manner in which he began the panel in the 1981 triptych *Desire (The Charterhouse)* (p 87). The artist set out to paint a robe, only to find that it appeared almost before he delineated it.

Hearts

A major theme in Dine's work—the Heart—developed from sets he designed in 1965 for Shakespeare's *A Midsummer Night's Dream*. For him the heart is a powerful emblem: the rounded, scarlet forms evoke not only childhood notions of romantic love but also the sexual organs. As such it is a neat combination of sacred and profane love "and strikes," he says, "a primitive chord." He is pleased with the extreme contrast of temporary looking straw and durable sheet metal in the fanciful sculpture *Nancy and I at Ithaca (Straw Heart)* (p 37), which provokes all manner of speculation. The conflict between context and texture recalls Meret Oppenheim's sexually-charged, fur-covered cup and saucer sculpture of 1936 (p 38), and the combination of heart and straw summons notions of rustic goings-on—love in a hayloft. This association of romantic love with a pastoral setting is firmly embedded in Western art in forms as varied as Dutch 17th-century portraiture and Shakespeare's plays. Dine gives this tradition a contemporary twist with the words of the title "Nancy and I" that more than hint at romantic companionship. "Ithaca" is the rural town in upstate New York that supplies the pastoral context.

Such idiosyncratic considerations aside, it is an austere work which dates from a period in which Dine painted very little. There was a group of now destroyed wire sculptures garnished with strands of rope and other bedraggled bits and pieces. Dine dedicated

Meret Oppenheim
Object 1936
fur-covered cup, saucer and
spoon
cup, 4⅜ diameter
saucer, 9⅜ diameter
spoon, 9 long
overall height 2⅞
Collection The Museum of
Modern Art, New York

Francis Picabia
L'Oeil Cacodylate 1921
oil and collage on canvas
57½ x 44⅞
Collection Musée National d'Art
Moderne

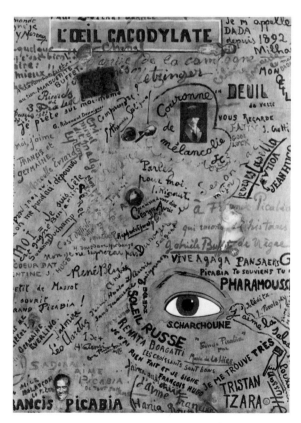

these proverbial "faint hearts" to John Peto, the 19th-century American master of still life who, through trompe l'oeil renderings of the detritus of civilization—battered books, letters and calling cards—composed a long, sustained song of "memento mori." Dine's affinity for the work of Peto is not difficult to fathom. He, too, favors unpretentious objects that have seen, to say the least, their fair share of action, and he is especially fond of those that have, in one way or another, become obsolete. Peto had his lost letters; Dine has his hand tools. This is not so much a manifestation of nostalgia as an acknowledgment that all things, whatever their current vitality, will eventually decay.

The greater part of Dine's oeuvre is characterized by a strong sense of *matière,* but the paintings and sculpture of the late 1960s are uncompromisingly austere. Although he was then living in London, they have a tangential relationship to the minimalist and process movements that were such notable features of the American art scene at that time. This was the beginning of a stringent analysis of his work which took the form of constructing very spare installations of sawhorses, planks, electric cables and light bulbs. It was, by his own account, a bleak period. By reducing the rich pattern of his art to a bare minimum of elements he contemplated a symbolic artistic suicide that would be followed by multiple reincarnations. "I can paint a lot of ways," he says, "and I had the idea that I could be another artist, that I could change my name and be an earth artist or

(p 40)
Painting a Fortress for the Heart
1981
acrylic on canvas
84 x 120
Collection Graham Gund

(p 41)
The Japanese Paper Company
1983
oil on canvas with objects
25 x 20¾ x 6
Courtesy The Pace Gallery

something like that, but keep on painting the way I was painting."

Such a radical transformation never took place. Instead, there was a very different inspiration for the ten ebullient Heart collages that came next. It was an encounter with Francis Picabia's 1921 collage, *L'Oeil Cacodylate* (p 38), which features an eye surrounded by signatures. It is not surprising that Dine opted for the heart as the central image of the series, but by the time he finished working on *Untitled (Tricky Teeth)*, 1970–71 (p 98) and its nine fellows, there was little, if anything, left of the spirit of Picabia. The sinister bleeding heart floating in the center is the only discordant note in otherwise colorful and cheerful images, a reflection of the artist's renewed confidence in this medium.

After his move to Vermont in 1971, Dine produced an extensive series of six- and seven-foot paintings in which the heart form occupies the entire canvas: the heart and the painting are synonymous. Various tools and objects are juxtaposed against these hearts, some of which have, as in *Poulenc*, violent overtones. In others, such as *I'm Painting with My Animals*, the quirky branches that lean protectively against the canvas are a veritable forest of amiable forms that convert the composition into a sumptuous landscape.

In late 1971 Dine continued to explore the Heart theme with another series, this time all six-feet square. The motif was then abandoned, as had been the Robe, for the best part of the next decade until he returned to it again in 1981,

a painful year. He was deeply concerned for a friend who was trying to recover from a severe mental breakdown. The paintings of that time, although shot through with flashes of color, are dark, heavily encrusted, and dominated by murky blackish hues. The color seems to be on the verge of extinction, as in *Painting a Fortress for the Heart* (p 40), in which the sunsetlike tones are threatened by the surrounding blacks. The picture virtually personifies the struggle between joy and pain, emotions that Dine "did not care to illustrate," preferring "to keep looking very hard [to] see if the paint itself can do the job."

There are many references to landscape in the Heart "program" of 1981. By deliberately applying the acrylic compound so thickly that it "crazed" when drying out—accelerated with electric heaters—Dine was able to recreate the tortured quality of the frost-cracked ground that he liked so much outside his Vermont studio. *A German Blackness* (p 110) evokes a more conventional landscape. A giant black heart, the symbol of love arrayed in mourning, hovers over a flaming apocalyptic landscape. The title refers to works of Lyonel Feininger, but Dine's constant worry about his ill friend resulted in imagery reminiscent of other, less comforting, northern-European painters, particularly the tortured netherworld of Hieronymous Bosch and the penitential hells of Mathias Grünewald.

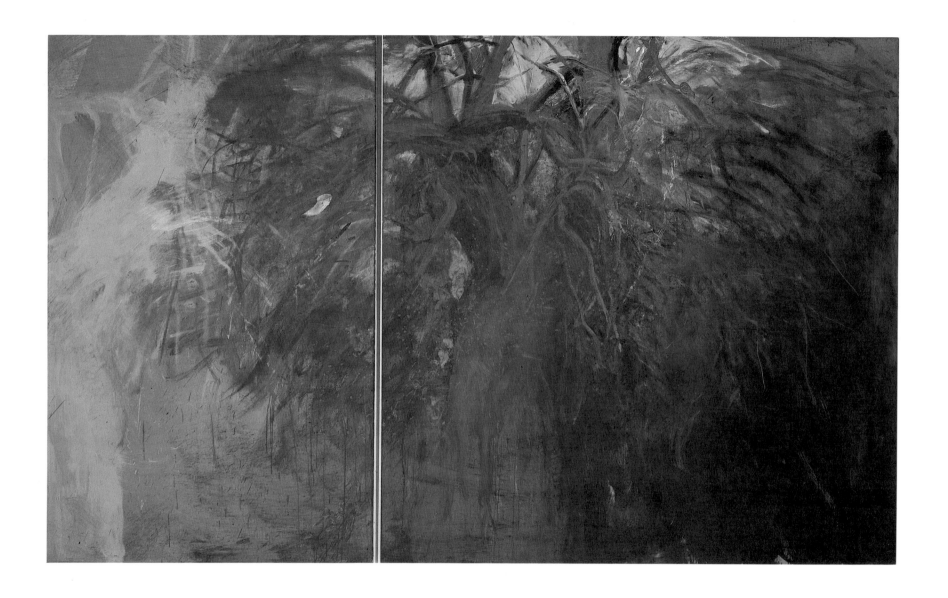

Red Tree, Flesh Tree, A Carnival Tree: The Painting 1980
oil on canvas
84 x 137¾ (2 panels)
Courtesy The Pace Gallery

Trees

It was not until 1980, with the Tree theme, that Dine addressed himself directly to his abiding and oft-stated love for landscape. The impetus was the small, aged, gnarled apple tree growing near the Vermont studio. At first he worked slowly in oils from an enlarged photograph, but he soon paid no attention to it. In *A Tree in the Shadow of Our Intimacy* (p 123) the tree explodes, ragged and expansive and quite unlike the solidly defined Hearts or the columnar Robes. Similarly, in all of the Tree paintings the blurred shapes of the branches lash out in every direction, and the whirling trunks appear to be propelled by an unknown centrifugal force. To Dine, the trees are a metaphor for the female torso, and the allusion is undeniable.

Nowhere is the sense of giddy motion more pronounced than in *A Tiger Lies at the Bottom of Our Garden* (p 124). The title refers to the beloved American tale of a little black boy and four threatening tigers who chase each other around and around a tree until finally they dissolve into butter. Such playful titles do not disguise Dine's continuing artistic growth: with the Tree paintings he finally leaves behind his assemblagist youth to confront his American and European expressionist peers and precursors. Paint alone now carries the message, and paint alone now makes the allusions and references. In the uncharacteristically asymmetrical work *Red Tree, Flesh Tree, A Carnival Tree: The Painting*

(p 42), a crimson tree spreads its flayed body beside the soft bulk of a pink tree. The first words of the title recall Piet Mondrian's elegant *Red Tree* of 1909–10, but the vascular forms of the painting itself are close relatives to the frantic bloodshot souls of James Ensor's expressionist paintings or de Kooning's ferocious *Woman II*.

Dine's expressionism is fully demonstrated in *Desire (The Charterhouse)*, a powerful triptych that features the tree motif flanked by a robe and a heart. The trio of forms seems to waver, as if viewed through the rising heat of their creation and Dine has commented on the almost spontaneous generation of the Robe image. Any sense of frenzy, however, is counteracted by considerable formal restraint. Other than the black, white and gray paint in this virtually monochromatic work, the only hues are the dirt and rubbish scooped from the studio floor. The composition is highly symmetrical—no mean feat in itself, given the basic disparity of the forms. The robe and tree are firmly anchored to the bottoms of their panels by their columnar configurations, and the heart is as securely moored by the curtain of paint that, dribbling to the foot of the canvas, echoes the wobbly verticals of its companions.

Dine has often repeated a single motif within one work, a device rooted in the "serial" method of composition that was popular in the 1960s. Recent experiments take a new direction: several themes play against each

43

The Black Crommelynck Gate
1981
acrylic on linen
84 x 168 (2 panels)
Courtesy The Pace Gallery

other within a single work. If *Desire (The Charterhouse)* presents an unexpectedly unified composition, the effect in another and slightly earlier "compound" piece is altogether different. *Painting (Cruising) (La Chasse)* (p 105) was a deliberate test. It features four motifs, of which only the Heart was a familiar Dine theme at the time. The others, a leaden Star of David, a hoary tree, and a hazy gate, are new. Furthermore, each motif is rendered specifically to accentuate its own intrinsic qualities: the Star of David is solid and geometric; the tree is brittle and disorderly and the gate is transparent and lacelike. The painting is an essay in clashing form, a pictorial lineup of Dine's personal options, a probe of the new against the tried to see which, if any, he will pursue. One theme, he says, will not be used again: the Star of David is "much too specific." The Gate and the Tree, however, have become significant features of his current repertoire.

Gates

The Gate theme of the early 1980s differs from Dine's others in almost every respect. It derives from a purely artistic context and not, like the others, from the everyday, basically American circumstances of the artist's life. Tools, robes, hearts and trees all have distinctly anthropomorphic characteristics and are basically volumetric, no matter how much they may otherwise vary. The gates, by contrast, are geometric and diaphanous: wrought iron tracery defines the spaces around, behind and through them. Dine deliberately chose this theme to express his determination to eliminate all references to the human figure in his work, a step closer to pure abstraction. This new image, inspired by the elegant 19th-century gate in front of master printer Aldo Crommelynck's Paris house, has a formality and sense of order that sets it apart from the unruly tree whose comrade-in-time it is. It also differs in its relationship to the picture plane. The solid, bulky forms of the robes, the hearts and the trees usually dominate the backgrounds against which they stand, and often obscure them. The tools, a somewhat different case, are set off by the discrepancies of their materials. The gates' relationship to their backgrounds is altogether more equivocal: the sparse outlines of their frameworks allow plenty of room for the background paint, which is almost more important than the form of the theme itself.

In *The Crommelynck Gate* (p 137) of 1981, one of the first fully realized paintings of the

theme, the scroll-like lines of the wrought iron are firmly delineated in all but a few areas, and the gate stretches across the full width of a thirteen-foot canvas, a rigid barrier at the edge of a swirling fog. Actual threat emanates from *The Black Crommelynck Gate* (p 45). Here the ironwork appears to phosphoresce, to be coiled ready to strike; passage through it would be fraught with peril. Dine had once before dealt, albeit obliquely, with the idea of dangerous passage in a bizarre 1965 sculpture, *The Hammer Doorway*, in which two attenuated hammers function as doorposts and the hammer heads as a vestigial lintel. This work dates from the austere period immediately following the first Robe paintings and Dine has rarely, if ever, produced a sparer image. Combining a sense of elegance with the notion of physical threat, it is an ancestor of Dine's most recent sculpture *The Crommelynck Gate with Tools* (p 143).

Created over a period of many months—an unusually long time for Dine —*The Crommelynck Gate with Tools* is a giant work, at least twice the size of its ostensible model and, as the title indicates, bristles with his familiar tools. The graceful curlicues of the original have been replaced with clamps, hammers, pliers and twisted pick handles as Dine firmly puts his stamp on the new image, taking it from the quiet anonymity of suburbia to the troubled frontiers of a surreal world. Further, heavy diagonal elements have been substituted for the original's delicate rectangular framework, making the upper part of the gate analogous with the shoulders of the Robe image. Echoes of the Heart form also can be detected in the arabesques of the ironwork. More significant than any formal shift, however, is the overall emotional effect of the new image for, despite the artist's witty sleights of hand and the ramshackle appearance of the sculpture, whimsicality is hardly its most notable characteristic. As in the paintings and drawings from which it evolved, *The Crommelynck Gate with Tools* is a forbidding monument, a barbed and prickly structure that denies rather than promises passage.

Looking back over Dine's career it is now apparent that, in responding to the spirit of irony and detachment that pervaded the art world of the early 1960s—the so-called Pop era—Dine was clamping down hard on what now seems to be the cardinal characteristic of his own artistic personality: a profound expressionism. The wit that informs so much of his work from this period is, more often than not, a thin veil that barely obscures highly personal, emotionally charged content. Commenting on the extreme emotionalism of his Happenings Dine once said "I do not think obsession is funny." Neither, he added, was "not being able to stop one's intensity." In an effort to distance himself from his predecessors, the abstract expressionists, and to control the passion with which he felt the need to make art,

Dine adopted the urbane mask of the assemblagist. He was a natural exponent of the technique and in such early works as *Lawnmower* and *Five Feet of Colorful Tools* he created masterpieces of the genre. But as the decade wore on Dine found the technique less and less apt for his purposes and an approach that had been, for a few years, the catalyst for creativity became a trap. At the same time that such comrades in Pop Art were refining and expanding their chosen forms, Dine found himself down something of a blind alley. Where introducing a tool to a painting once had the effect on him of "hitting a home run" he now felt that he couldn't "just push one more beautiful object around."

Having physically removed himself from New York and, for a while from America, in the early 1970s Dine turned his back on the technique with which he had established his reputation. He made, he said, "a huge amount of drawings but not a lot of paintings. It was a period when . . . it seemed I could do a lot with my hands that I didn't think I could do before. I was learning to sit . . . and draw rather than make the grand gesture all the time." He all but banished the "non-art object" from his repertoire—although it is debatable whether, by that time, such an object existed—and by concentrating on drawing subjected himself to the kind of discipline he had hitherto avoided. In doing so he made, for the time being, a complete break with his past and with his erstwhile peers. Dine had been a "young Turk" in the Pop generation, but as his drawing and painting style developed in the 1970s it became clear that his new figurative and expressionist work heralded a shift in the art world at large. A new generation of younger painters was exploring aspects of figurative Expressionism and Dine suddenly and unexpectedly found himself in the role of something of an elder statesman. From his own perspective, he was simply giving mature form to ideas he had always, throughout a long, difficult and often bitter apprenticeship sought to express. From another perspective it is clear that Dine can be regarded as a leading figure of the revitalized expressionist movement and that his work now belongs firmly within the greater context of the American expressionist tradition. Dine's themes, however, continue to lie literally and figuratively at the center of his art. It seems likely that familiar ones will be recycled, and that from time to time new ones will appear. When they do they will be as unexpected as their predecessors, and will almost certainly be linked to his own life experiences. The origin of an ostensible motif may now be of less significance than in the past, but there cannot be a separation between it, the artist and his technique: the theme is the paint; the paint is the theme; the theme is Dine; Dine is the paint.

TOOLS

Associations feel simply explicit, although that may have only to do with the fact that one's information of the Dine family's involvement with classic hardware *tools*—they had a store in Cincinnati—is both provocative and secure. It was the substantial factor in the family's economy. The young artist worked occasionally in the store relating. Tools are both insistent and functional, suggest a complexly ranging physical environment and also keep the stability of 'home,' are familiar and strange.

He obviously thought about them a good deal and if the hearts were and are the emotional weather of his life, the robes the attempt to see oneself not only as others might see one but as that sight given back, then tools are somehow what one does and can do. Or, perhaps better, one can recognize things are done and these things do them. The occasional presence of a glove in the company, in *Untitled 1973 (Monument)* (p 55) for example, makes clear the transitional factor of agency, the who does what with what. The tools are forever. At times they are far more than what their function, taken literally, will provide for and two hammers with immensely elongated handles become *The Hammer Doorway* (p 54). How can one confidently propose this is simply a metaphor for what hammers can make, or a play on the visual suggestions of a hammer head, or even some threatening possibility there is to be violence 'inside'?

At times the tools are codifying anchor for a reality—the artist's whimsical and perceptive understanding of the powers of order—that includes a solid emphasis upon all manner of literal and abstract things, *Five Feet of Colorful Tools,* crowding in all respects the top of this painting "with board and objects," has as much practical density as people waiting for a subway and as curiously evident a sense of time as old coats hung in a closet. All the echoic layering is, one would think, a good deal more than simple memories. If "a place for everything and everything in its place" were ever to have a chance in this world, this painting would still come to haunt it. The act of hanging things up, putting things back, respecting things the way they were, is all wound in here in a way neither ironic nor pragmatic. Even who hung them up is very much a question.

Still the presence of tools is remarkably particular and common, even when they are in situations of transformation *(The Hammer Doorway)* or, in some sense, visually incomplete *Pliers* (from *Untitled Tool Series)*. They also take place in the painting, drawing, assemblage, etc., in a very matter-of-fact way, upright, either sitting firmly on bottom margin or plane, or else hung in like manner. Clearly they are the things that can and do work, however various, echoing and unlocated one's own relation to them may sometimes be. RC

Big Black Work Wall 1961
oil on canvas with objects
72¾ x 108⅛ x 4½ (2 panels)
Private collection, London

The Black Shovel 1962
oil on canvas with objects
and earth
wall panel, 96 x 38
box, 12 x 38 x 12
Courtesy Sonnabend Gallery

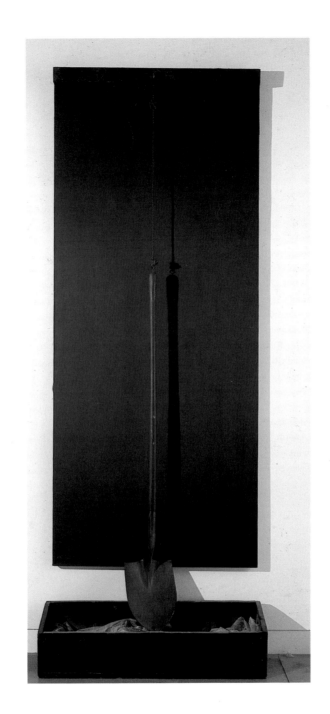

Small Shower

Small Shower 1962
oil with object on canvas
48 x 36
Collection Mr. and Mrs. Morton
G. Neumann

There's no difference between shower heads
and axes and hammers; they're all
metaphorical, obvious stand-ins for human
things. I began by fastening the shower head to
the top of the canvas and then painted around
it. At the time I was using flesh-colored paint
as a joke, as a kind of studied dumbness. I
painted the water spraying out of the shower
head in black and white and then used flesh
color straight from the tube. I found the very
beautiful white enamel letters in New York, in
hardware stores on the Lower East Side. I was
more naive, then, about what I wanted to do; I
liked using cool deadpan lettering a lot more
than I do now. I'm much more "hot" today.

The Hammer Doorway 1965
cast aluminum (unique)
78 x 40½ x 7½
Collection Gene R. Summers

Untitled 1973 (Monument)
pencil, watercolor and collage
on paper
22½ x 30½
Collection The Washington Art
Consortium: Cheney Cowles
Memorial State Museum,
Spokane; Museum of Art,
Washington State University,
Pullman; Tacoma Art Museum,
Tacoma; the Henry Gallery,
University of Washington,
Seattle; the Western Gallery,
Western Washington State
University, Bellingham; the
Whatcom Museum of History
and Art, Bellingham

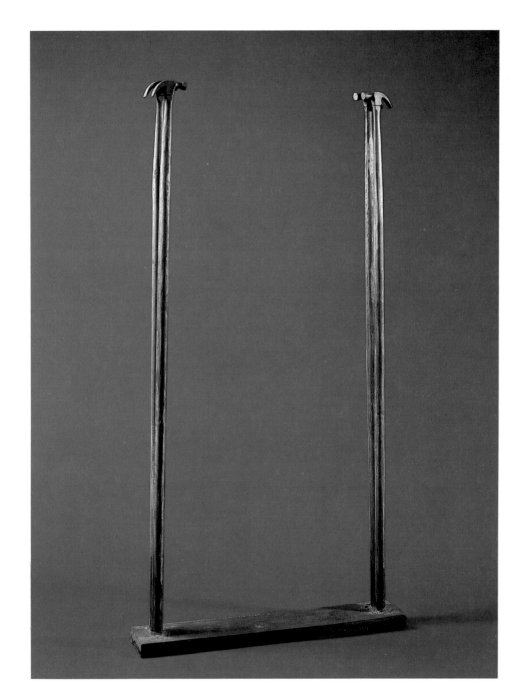

55

The Art of Painting No. 2   1973
enamel and acrylic on canvas
with objects
48 x 180 (5 panels)
Collection The Art Museum,
Princeton University
Given by Stanley J. Seeger, Jr.
in memory of Helen B. Seeger
through the Helen B. Seeger
Fund

Objects that hang from a cold sky against
gestural grass—this was done at the same time
as *Our Life Here*, and is really *about* painting. I
bought twenty-four aerosol bombs of blue
Rustoleum, kind of like the Vermont sky, took
the valves off and shoved in nails which
exploded them all over the canvas. When it
dried I put on another coat and while the final
coat was wet I made the grass part with acrylic
paint and it all dried together.

Ten years later the fan in my studio is still
blue and surely it's in my lungs too.

5-Bladed Saw

Pliers

Dry-Wall Hammer

(p 62)
Hoof Nipper

(p 62)
Oil Can

(p 63)
C Clamp

(p 63)
Brace and Bit

(from *Untitled Tool Series*)
1973
charcoal and graphite on paper
25⅝ x 19⅞
Collection The Museum of
Modern Art, New York
Gift of the Robert Lehman
Foundation, Inc.

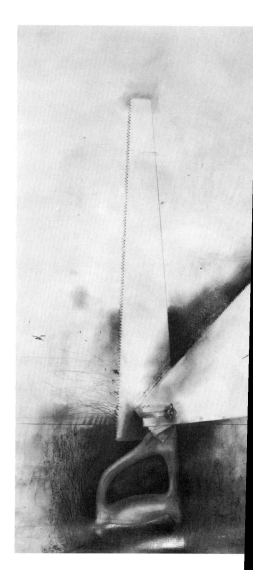

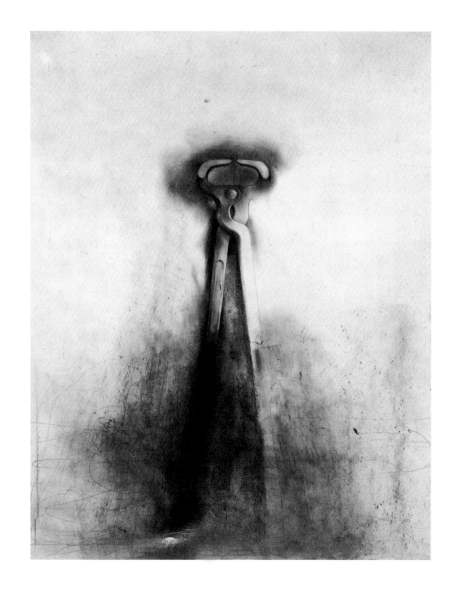 

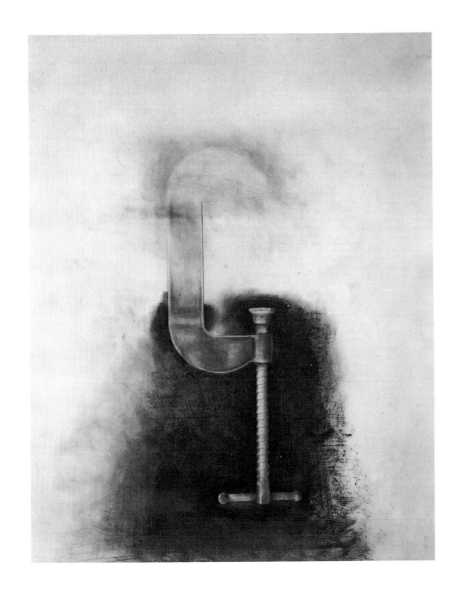 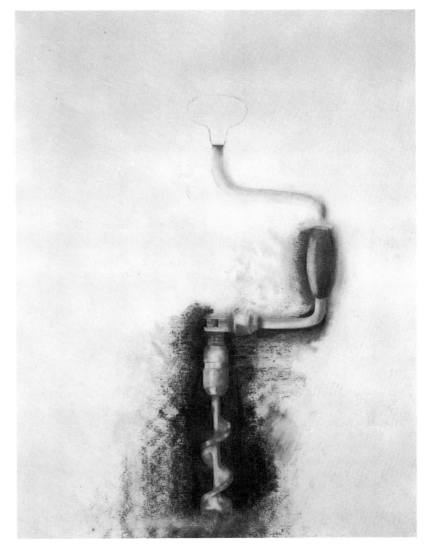

63

Untitled 1974

Untitled 1974
charcoal and gouache on paper
42 x 60
Private collection

I really did this picture so I could make charcoal marks on a paper surface, and they mean as much as the shape of the tool. I wanted a clean tool for my drawing, no involvement with anyone else's mystery. I came across this two-man saw in Vermont, as beautiful a piece of sculpture as any objet trouvé. Even though it was brand new, it's a kind of 19th-century object, and about as far as I wanted to go with old-fashioned tools. I don't care about the nobility of old utilitarian objects.

I wasn't interested in depicting the act of work, only in the tool itself, as sculpture. My tools refer to people without having to deal with a human presence; they aren't monuments to American workers.

Untitled 1974

Untitled 1974
charcoal and pastel on paper
36 x 30
Collection Mrs. Julius E. Davis

The pitchfork came from the same farm supply place in Vermont as the two-man saw. I liked the challenge of drawing it because it was not like drawing a still-life object on a table. I wanted to present it as an object in dark, indeterminate space. The tines were particularly difficult to draw. They emerge from the blackness as highlights.

To get the frontality and sharp contours I like in my tool drawings, I place the object against the paper and run a pencil around it. Then I place it across the room and draw from it. This way I set the stage for a rigid, formalist picture. The tracing doesn't say anything so you still have to lie by draftsmanship, which pleases me no end. It lets me meander in and around the shape of the object in an atmospheric way, a romantic way, a black way. It forces me to invent.

Axe

Axe 1975
pastel and spray enamel
on paper
69¼ x 22
Collection Nancy M. O'Boyle

Shovel 1975
pastel and spray enamel
on paper
60 x 12½
Collection Mr. and Mrs. E. A.
Bergman

Here's a good example of the liberties I take.
The axe handle is obviously elongated, a
personality, I suppose, in a pretty primitive
way. Like the pitchfork, the picture describes
an object in light. I use light in the way that
William Blake or Samuel Palmer would
understand.

ROBES

If clothes can make the man, these *robes* exist in a place that is neither quite one nor the other. They stand foursquare through the years, sometimes primarily an outline but always with an intrinsic volume much as if an invisible man were their occupant. In that way they are like houses for a particular imaginal body, a self embodied in a 'self-portrait,' which sees always what it is either doing or what is being done to it. The heads are missing because the plane of the painting has no room for them. They would fall off like those ships once were thought to, having come to the edge of the ocean. But more, the torso is under the cloth, not apart from it. There are no necks or hands, for example.

It is also interesting that they are robes, not suits, or coats or other modes of clothing. It seems that a robe, a bathrobe or dressing gown as it may variously be called, makes a dignity possible between a state of usual dress and undress. It is both intimate and intently formal. So, too, is the repetitive stance, faced to a presumable mirror, taking a clearly determined look.

Initially it all seems playful or at least open to an employment of possibilities which are more fact of the situation resolved on than what's brought to it. *Double Isometric Self-Portrait (Serape)* and *Self-Portrait Next to a Colored Window* have each a double play on any presumed fact of person, not only this one. In short, the same is not the same but always different.

It thinks apart from itself, by objectifying mechanical agency in one instance (it holds *itself* together, thank you (twice)) and, in the other, what's alongside so defines it that there's no getting out of it at all (a dotted line no less). Another work of this year (1964) has much the same intrinsic humor, *Charcoal Self-Portrait in a Cement Garden* (p 75), the garden a few fragmented bits of funereal oddment or possibly pedestals for birdbaths—but nothing, in fact, very funny at all as the figure behind them finds its dimension and substance somehow located by these squat, small solidnesses. Its belt, for example, has become curiously persuaded.

A little more than ten years later one finds much changed, although the apparent form has survived. Yet one might say that in this work, all of it, content is never more than an extension of form(s). Paradoxically, that formula can be read either way since the terms prove inseparable, at least in thought. And while this work is not overtly intellectual exercise, any of it, it is deeply thoughtful, thinks through feeling. Now there is nothing in front of the image, no term of inherent reflection. All that happens, or that has happened, is manifest directly on the face of what one sees. There one is, whoever, and again as with the surface of the hearts—or literal person or painting—what happens happens here, and is that information, happy, sad, all the same. And all comes closer. RC

Red Robe with Hatchet (Self-Portrait)

*Red Robe with Hatchet
(Self-Portrait)* 1964
oil on canvas with objects
60 x 60 x 23
(87 x 60 overall)
Sydney and Frances Lewis
Collection

This is from the summer of 1964 in East
Hampton when I began working on my first
show of Robe pictures, but I wasn't free enough
then to improvise, so it's quite rigid in its
definition. I probably visualized the axe, the log
and the bathrobe as an extension of myself—a
self-portrait.

Actually, I never wear a bathrobe. I began
to draw from a real one only in 1979 in
Jerusalem when Nancy photographed me in it
so I would get the folds right. There's some sort
of primitive abstraction in the painting of it that
is slightly embarrassing to me now. The log
was found in a lumber yard; it had been there a
long time and was used for cutting other logs.

If the picture has to do with anything it
might be about cutting, which is implicit in
using an axe. I've always loved them, the way
they look, what they can do, their menacing
quality ("I'd like to sharpen my axe") and see
them as a metaphor for many things.

Charcoal Self-Portrait in a Cement Garden 1964
charcoal and oil on canvas with objects
108³⁄₁₆ x 47¹⁵⁄₁₆ x 27
Collection Allen Memorial Art Museum, Oberlin College, Fund for Contemporary Art

This charcoal was done in the summer of 1964. The busted objects in front of it were found at the local Agway, a garden and farm supply store. I have always been attracted to so-called vanitas objects because they relate to the Academy and to Chardin. I always seem to make references through paint or objects to an older art. It's a link to my past.

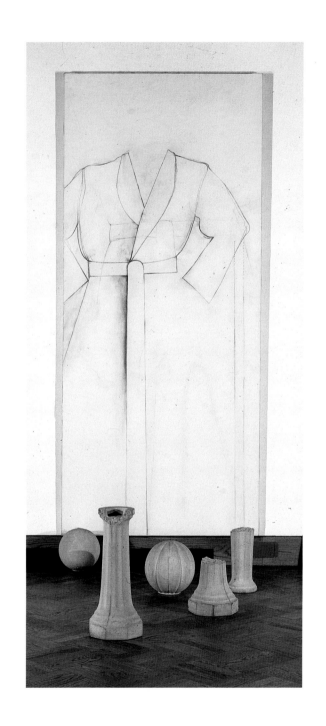

Four Robes Existing in This Vale of Tears

Red Robe #2   1964
oil and collage on canvas
84 x 60
Collection Richard Brown
Baker, Courtesy Yale University
Art Gallery

(p 78)
*Four Robes Existing in This Vale
of Tears*   1976
oil on panel
80 x 144 (4 panels)
Collection Gene R. Summers

I had not painted a "robe" for years until 1976.
I had moved on because I had other concerns
and was involved in other things. I had been
drawing like crazy in the 70s, and also making
those paintings with tools. What brought me
back were the figure drawings made every day
in 1975–76. I didn't want to paint the figure, but
was quite happy to draw it, and the robe was
how I could use all my knowledge of drawing.
They became different—less involved with me
personally, and more about making a painting
with the robe as a subject. Also, I wanted to use
oil paint more carefully.

Cardinal

Cardinal   1976
oil on canvas
108 x 72
Sydney and Frances Lewis
Collection

This is a really red robe. It is also a glowing
object in a field. I was really in love with the oil
paint. I corrected, painted and built up that red
against the green ground—you can't miss with
that combination.

Light Comes upon the Old City
1979
oil on canvas
78¾ x 48
Collection Mr. and
Mrs. Sidney Kahn

Tonight There is Weather   1979
oil on canvas
102½ x 81

Balcony

Balcony 1979
oil on canvas
102¼ x 81
Collection Philadelphia Museum
of Art
Gift of the Friends of the
Philadelphia Museum of Art

I had a big book in my studio open to the Manet painting because I love it. I don't like the figure but I *love* the balcony. I spent months fiddling with my balcony, trying to get the angles right.

Note: The reference is to Edouard Manet's *The Balcony*, 1869 Collection Musée National du Louvre

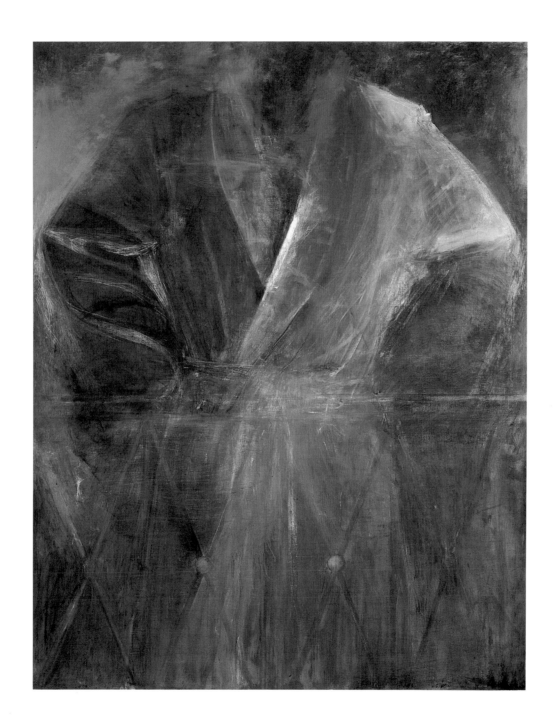

Desire (The Charterhouse)

Desire (The Charterhouse) 1981
acrylic on linen
84 x 252 (3 panels)

This is very expressionistic and in some way seems to grip those who have seen it. I didn't set out to do that, but it's a good example of what I know in painting. I had wanted to make a three-panel work but I wasn't sure what they would have on them. In fact, the robe just appeared; it evolved because of knowledge, of what I have stored. Also, I wanted to make it black and white, something I hadn't probably specifically done before. I did not yearn to use color but I found color against the black and white. For instance, in the heart panel there is a kind of tan. I threw dirt and dust from the floor onto the canvas and it stuck and gave a color that wasn't pigment, so it kept the painting black and white. It was an important addition, and it thrilled me.

It's called *Desire (The Charterhouse)* because it was painted in Charterhouse Square in London in the fall of 1981. Someone wrote to me after seeing the exhibition catalogue: "*Desire* is your new power, right?" The word came to me after the painting was finished. I was experiencing a state of psychic desire, which really got to me. But this kind of desire is not specifically desiring someone or something; it is the state of desiring to remove the state of loneliness. So, in the same way the robe appeared, the title appeared. Now *Desire* has become a way to make titles so that I can change and enrich my subject matter and not have to put it under a category like the Heart or Robe.

Jerusalem Nights   1979
acrylic on canvas
96 x 95½ (2 panels)
Collection Paul and
Camille Oliver Hoffmann

This was painted in my bedroom in Jerusalem in 1979. The room was very tall but quite small, so the bed was a great place to sit and paint from. I suspended two big rolls of canvas from the ceiling and taped my brushes to long sticks. I had been laboring over oil paintings all summer, but for this I bought black and white acrylic and used it quickly. It was very fresh. The painting looks as if one of the panels is in front of the other, which is because they overlapped, so I had the stretcher built that way.

Painting Around Mount Zion
1979
oil on canvas
71 x 173 (4 panels)
Collection Akron Art Museum

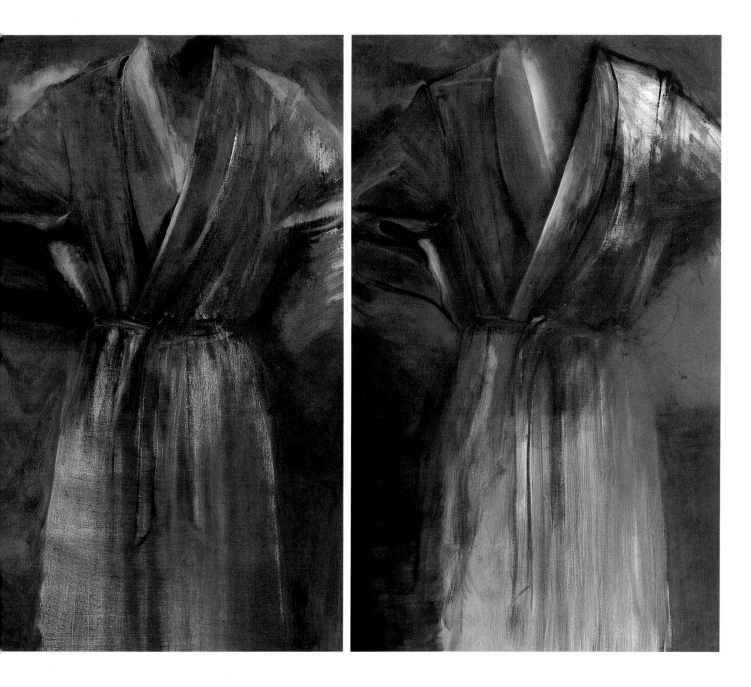

HEARTS

Just as one's self will serve as constant in a world of otherwise shifting reference, a *heart* is sign that one can care, that there is a consistent presence of feeling. In a curious way this heart is neither inside nor outside oneself but, rather, exists in a hieratic determination of its own possibility, and so lives in a place that can be as powerfully singular and remote as the moon or as physically evident and contained as one's own hands, feet and head.

This heart is an imagination, of course. One knows the actual heart looks not at all like those most familiar from the iconographic slogans of Valentine's Day—which seems itself an invention from faint root except that there must be one day on which, unequivocally, hearts triumph. *Have a heart . . .*

It would be an error, however, to presume that these specific hearts are either symbolic or ultimately abstract. They are far more like weather, a shifting presence that has faces but is not itself a fixed content. More apt then to call them, among other things, a ground or context which serves as means for feeling out the possibilities of what is going on.

The insistent echoes of this image must have been delight to an artist so remarkably open to language and its powers. One can trust the associations here of everything from 'A heart as big as all outdoors' to 'hardhearted' or 'brokenhearted' or simply, 'The heart of the matter.' The language of the titles is a useful evidence of how variously this 'heart' can find occasion, whether it prove *I'm Painting with My Animals,* where a veritable outside comes in to lean against the heart, or *Nancy and I at Ithaca (Straw Heart)* with its backward pun upon *The Wizard of Oz.* The point is that it does not stand for something else nor has it only a force determined by what it means, or wants to. As a presence it gathers resonance as would a cross or flag, even without information. Playing literalizing objects against it, or determining it as object also (as must be the case in *Nancy and I* with "sheet iron and straw, 60 x 70 x 12½), leave it much as a whale on a beach, persistently itself in whatever locus.

Therefore what changes is all else, and that is why one does engage in *Romancing in Late Winter* (p 111) and *Painting a Fortress for the Heart.* It is an elegant, fructifying image, often voluptuous in its provocatively paired French curves. Yet one feels the pain and frustration its emblem has incessantly borne with it, pierced with arrows, split in two, blackened, cracked. It wears its colors bravely. RC

Untitled (Gloves)
Untitled (Tricky Teeth)

Untitled (Gloves) 1970–71
charcoal, pastel and collage on
paper with objects
60 x 40
Collection Stuart and
Anne Robinowitz

(p 98)
Untitled (Tricky Teeth)
1970–71
pastel, zinc and collage on paper
60 x 42
Collection Mr. and
Mrs. Fred Carr

(p 99)
I'm Painting with My Animals
1971
acrylic on canvas with objects
72 x 69

Both of these were made in London in the fall and winter of 1970–71. I had just been to the Trocadero in Paris where I "saw" the Picabia with an eye painted on it and signed by many people in different kinds of type. Very alive objects. What interested me were all the different elements, and I put together a group of pictures by pasting a heart in the middle of each one, and showed them at the Sonnabend Gallery in New York that spring.

The bleeding heart in the center of these two works had already been used as a motif in the costumes and sets for a theater production of *The Picture of Dorian Gray*. It was never produced, but I got an illustrated book out of it, and that's where this bleeding heart came from. I made a gouache of the heart, it was reproduced lithographically, and then I cut them out to use as the central piece. The heart on *Tricky Teeth* was cut from a gray lithographic plate. I thought the real gloves in *Gloves* were particularly poignant because they are stand-ins for hands. The rest of the picture comes from the floor of my studio. I'm always aware of what's on the floor, wherever I'm

working. I leave things there intentionally, walk on them, spit on them, more crap drops on them, and maybe pastel dust rubs off on them. I trust accidents, which is why I like what falls on the studio floor, and it becomes grist for my mill.

I don't remember why I called the picture *Tricky Teeth*. At the time I was very close to the poets Ted Berrigan and Ron Padgett. Padgett is very much aware, as I am, of using found objects. I was writing a lot of poetry and letters to them, and this title probably came from a comic, or someone just wrote it to me. I haven't written poems since that time.

96

I'm Painting with My Animals
Coming in the Sun

Coming in the Sun 1971
acrylic on canvas with objects
74 x 77
Collection Byron and
Eileen Cohen

We moved to a little farm in Vermont in the
spring of 1971. There was no studio so I set up
an army tent, sank two poles in the ground to
use as an easel, and painted outside for the first
time ever. Those sticks in *I'm Painting with My
Animals* were used by an animal to make a
burrow of sorts. It was a house, just there in my
meadow, from a long time ago.

I had found an old lawnmower and used
it for *Coming in the Sun*. The painting is about
landscape and about the way the sun felt on my
body. It was the first time I used a single-image
heart on this scale. Before that there were three
double-heart paintings from the summer of
1970 in England, but they had a certain amount
of insouciance which I would like to correct
now because they weren't all that well
observed.

Poulenc

Poulenc 1971
acrylic on canvas with objects
72 x 72

After painting outside in that summer of 1971 in Putney, I built a small studio, heavily insulated against the cold, for the winter. I wanted to make a group of paintings six-feet square and *Poulenc* was one of eight. I was listening to Poulenc's music and I also like the way "Poulenc" looks, so I wrote his name on the picture. The saw was a Vermont accoutrement, nothing to do with Poulenc— they are both about *me*, about what tools mean, in some unconscious way. There are months, and sometimes years, when I never look at them, never think of them, but then they get to me.

My family were immigrants, hardware store owners on a very simple level. My grandpa, who raised me, thought he was a carpenter—he fixed things and made all kinds of things, but he wasn't a very good craftsman. He did it with such bravado, such self-confidence, that we believed in him. He let me play with his tools, but I think I would have had the same obsession if no one in my family had had anything to do with these primary objects. They are the link with our past, the human past, the hand.

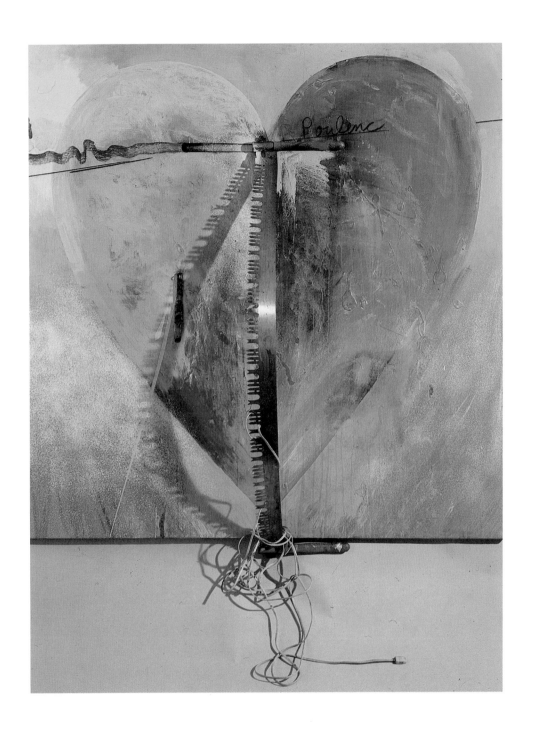

Painting (Cruising) (La Chasse)

Painting (Cruising)
(La Chasse) 1981
acrylic on canvas with objects
72 x 243¾ (4 panels)
Collection Mr. and Mrs. Asher
B. Edelman

I love this painting almost as much as anything I have ever done, except for *Desire (The Charterhouse)*. The act of cruising was what I was doing here, cruising my themes and cruising as a painter. That is, I was taking chances with unknown things and literally, physically, taking chances in the painting. This was a sort of random search for that sensation.

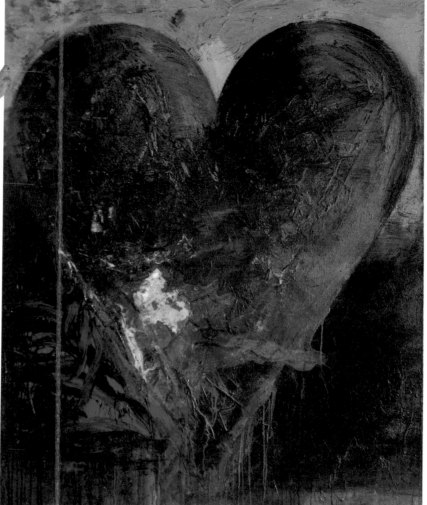

Blue Clamp 1981
acrylic on canvas with object
84 x 96
Collection Mr. and Mrs. Harry
W. Anderson

(p 110)
A German Blackness 1981
acrylic on canvas
96 x 84
Collection Douglas S. Cramer

(p 111)
Romancing in Late Winter 1981
acrylic on canvas
96 x 107½
Courtesy The Pace Gallery

This was the first time I had used a real tool for a long, long time. I chose it, not because it was a clamp, but because it was a beautiful piece of blue, a great blue, an industrial blue. It is a distraught painting that has to do with my landscape. I can't ever dictate what people will read into my work, but to say "the heart is being clamped by the blue clamp" is not right. All it really meant was putting a blue piece there that wasn't of paint. It didn't have any more intention than a stroke of paint except that it was another object—simply a piece of cast iron dipped in industrial blue paint, and that's all.

The Wall and the Fence
The Fence

In the fall of 1982 I was in London working every day in a foundry casting sculptures, but it wasn't happening fast enough. I missed color so I started to make some paintings. Nancy was in America and I was alone. We have a terrific little studio which was built about 1850, the time of the Great Exhibition when artists painted big pictures. There was an abandoned house overlooking the courtyard, and I thought the branches of a tree in the back would be great to use in a painting. So one night I went out with my cutters and lopped them off. Nancy was appalled. I used those branches coming out of six or seven paintings.

I hadn't combined objects with paint since 1975, and it was also good to get back to oil paint. The colors are so superb it's hard to understand why anyone would want to use acrylic, but I do because it is expedient and tough. The glowing colors give these paintings a tough Russian modernist look, like Jawlensky.

When I was working on *The Wall and the Fence* I'd come down every night—my studio is just below my bedroom—to have a look at it, and sometimes pause to paint a bit. Some evenings I painted in the dark—the studio has a proper skylight—not because I wanted a blindfold but because in the dim light I could see enough of the general contours to make clean changes. *The Fence* is a truly horizontal painting, five vertical panels with a tree branch between each one. It has no beginning or end. It's less complicated than *The Wall and the Fence,* more like a picture to be read, and it's a bit more open, with more white ground. I guess it's about transparency and how light, air and color affect things.

My color is always subjective. It has only been descriptive a few times, in the still lifes of the 1970s. I never really think about painting atmosphere, but what I do think about is sharpening my draftsmanship and about the power of objects.

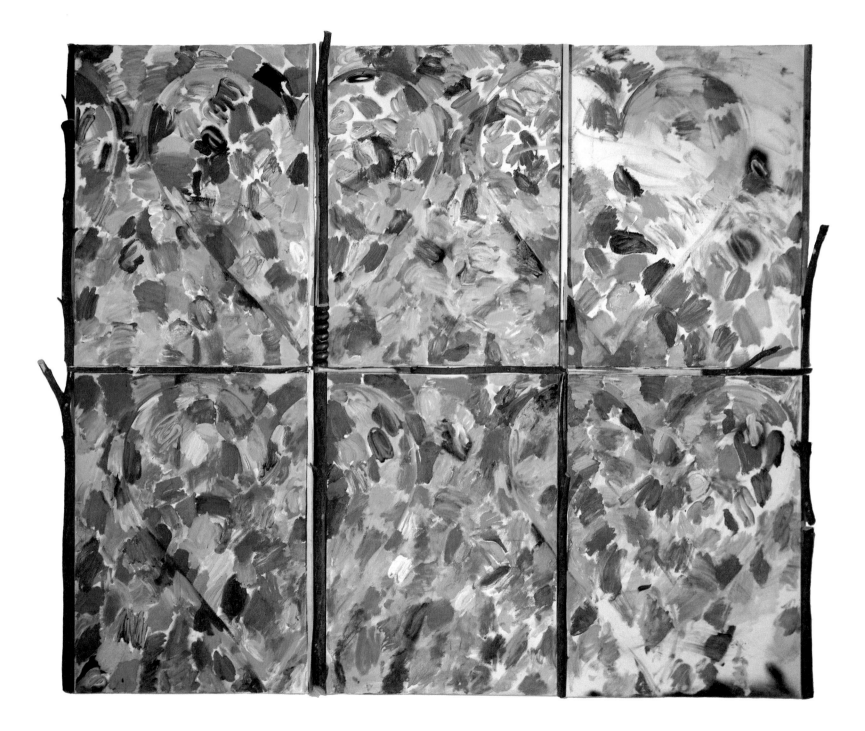

The Death at South Kensington
(October)

The Death at South Kensington, 2nd Version
(Piñon)

The Death at South Kensington
(October) 1983
oil on canvas with objects
60½ x 87¼
Collection Eileen Rosenau

This painting refers to the death, in the fall of 1983, of a friend who threw himself in front of a train at the South Kensington tube station in London.

I had started to make a group of small, formal, very beautifully painted works, but instead found myself making menacing paintings with axes and sticks. What began as colorful paintings soon became dark, brooding images full of earth tones—me in a black frame of mind, "Mr. Depression." It seemed impossible to finish this picture. My back hurt and so did everything else. The packers were coming, it was still wet, and the branches were sticking out wildly. I finally realized that it was my way of talking to my dead friend.

I think I made the heart and hand work together. The hand was taken from another of my paintings, *Lessons in Nuclear Peace,* which I had originally found in a book of paintings by survivors of Hiroshima, a hand dissolving as it was burning.

This painting (p 146) is more elaborate than the first version, with two added images, the burning chair and the tree. The color is more intense and primary, and is less depressing but in some ways more scary. I was still speaking about my dead friend.

114

Dine painting in his London
studio in the fall of 1983.
Photograph: Nancy Dine

Four Hearts of Sidney Close
1983
oil on canvas with objects
36½ x 29½ x 9½
Collection Milly and Arnold
Glimcher

TREES

There seems always an emphasis upon the singular, the one. Even in a cluster of tools, for example, it is their particularity as single objects that determines the nature of their company. It is a feeling that they have come together, as people might in some public situation, each from some specific circumstance or use.

There is, in fact, an anthropomorphic disposition in many of the images but it is not an enlargement of their proposed value, by presumption of human attributes. Rather they are seen intently, intensely, in ways that make of them precise human contexts and evocations.

Of all the themes variously engaged, only the *trees* might be said to have no necessarily human origin or invention. Certainly the tools and the hearts are each artifacts that have no meaning apart from how one may use them. Again, the image of the heart has finally little to do with that physical organ it so faintly represents, however closely it may relate to an imagined heart's crucial significance to human life itself. So too with the robes and gates.

However, the language of the titles insists equally upon this relation for the trees: *Red Tree, Flesh Tree, A Carnival Tree: The Painting; A Tree in the Shadow of Our Intimacy; A Tiger Lies at the Bottom of Our Garden.* Much as a figure approaching or else loomingly present, the trees are central in each image. Either one looks up to them, or sees them directly ahead, so to speak, in a scale significantly larger than one's own. In that respect they are as dense with imminent human information as might be any actual human figure.

Very probably this fact invests the appearance of these trees, this tree (one would feel them to be a single tree, in shifting perspectives but always forefront), with echoes of a human torso or, more aptly, the look of the robe images with open space of the neck a marked parallel to the effect of the tree's crotch. It is particularly evident in *Desire (The Charterhouse)*, with its three panels of robe, tree, and heart respectively. Someone is insistently *here,* one wants to say, whether it be the artist, the onlooker, or the image found in the work itself. One feels witness to a presence which will momently say much more than its brooding silence will now permit.

To see the trunks of trees, the entangled, twisted branches, as a myriad of human detail (hair, arms, fingers, bodies) would be a familiar nightmare of children, for whom the thing must be the thing as one sees it, without relief. *A Tiger Lies at the Bottom of Our Garden* plays complexly on a diversity of text, both in language and in image, confronting any possibility of secure resolution or containment with unremitting ambivalence. So does a reflecting 'tree of life' become the life itself. RC

A View in Sologne (for Pep and Aldo)

A View in Sologne (for Pep and Aldo) 1980
oil on canvas
84 x 152 (2 panels)

Nancy and I went back to New York for Christmas in 1980 (we had been in France and England printing etchings) where I worked on this painting. That autumn I had seen three ancient oaks in Windsor Great Park, but I made the two trees without photographs. The Crommelyncks have a house in Sologne that I have never seen, but I thought I would make something like a handshake across the sea for them.

A Tree in the Shadow of Our Intimacy
A Tiger Lies at the Bottom of Our Garden

A Tree in the Shadow of Our Intimacy 1980
oil on canvas
82½ x 84½
Collection Mr. and Mrs. Aron B. Katz

(p 124)
A Tiger Lies at the Bottom of Our Garden 1980
oil on canvas
82½ x 84½

(p 125)
Blue 1980
oil on canvas
80 x 96 (3 panels)
Courtesy The Pace Gallery

I passed this apple tree for years. In the winter it was just like a piece of sculpture. One of my kids took a photo of it which I enlarged and painted from. I couldn't get the piece to work, and I made four single trees, one of which is *A Tree in the Shadow of Our Intimacy*. I tried to use oil paint and build it up slowly, but it was a real struggle. The trees were deeply moving, mainly because I struggled so much with them. Finally, I said to myself, "This is ridiculous. You can't just sit here in this constipated way and paint from a photograph of a tree. You have to be yourself." So I painted *A Tiger Lies at the Bottom of Our Garden* in about a week.

Rose and Grey

Rose and Grey 1980
oil on canvas
82½ x 84½
Collection Gene R. Summers

(p 128)
*The Blue of Autumn with a Red
Light* 1980
oil on canvas
82½ x 84½
Collection Gene R. Summers

(p 129)
Tree (The Kimono) 1980
pastel, charcoal and enamel
on paper
71 x 60
Collection Museum of Fine Arts,
Boston, anonymous gift

This is a scraped-down tree painting. I scraped it until the paint started to run down, and it became a bit muddy, rose and gray rather than red and brown. It's the sparest of the Tree paintings. There may be a female form lurking in it. If such images do exist in my work it interests me. In fact, such mythological and psychological references, when they appear to me or to others, are wonderful gifts, bonuses.

Double Green Diptych
A Richly Grown Drawing

Double Green Diptych 1980–82
pastel, charcoal and enamel
on paper
35⅜ x 70½

(p 132)
A Richly Grown Drawing 1980
pastel, charcoal and enamel
on paper
45½ x 65½

I combined a series of monotypes to make double tree images. I like serial imagery. *A Richly Grown Drawing* had some strips added in the middle to make it go together formally. I kept *Double Green Diptych* in my studio and worked on it for three years. Somehow it became a white tree on a green ground. These strange trees take me back to my childhood fears of darker things, so working in this way exorcises my demons and keeps me in touch with unreality. I take on a lot of other people's agony and exorcise it through painting. In a primitive society I would maybe be a shaman, one of those guys who is a hit man for an unconscious civilization.

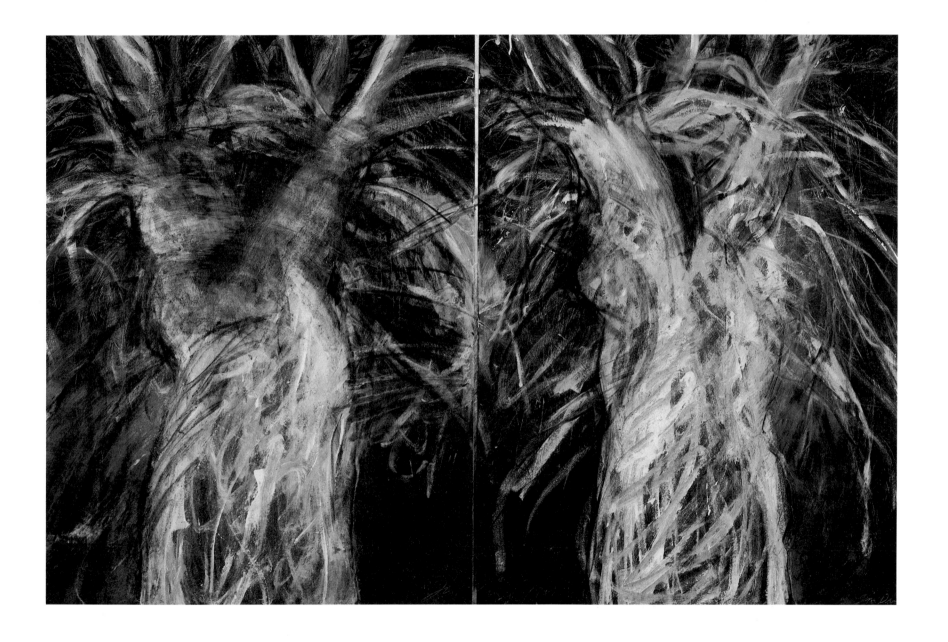

Blue 1981
engraving and hardground
etching
printed by Mitchell Friedman
and Nicholas Dine
40¾ x 54 (2 sheets)
Courtesy Pace Editions Inc.

Swaying in the Florida Night
1983
etching and engraving
printed by Robert Townsend
47 x 70½
Courtesy Pace Editions Inc.

GATES

There seems some change in preoccupations here. For one thing, the *gates*—or more truly the gate, since the images come from one factual gate, as the titles make clear—are a new presence in the iconography. Too, they, along with the trees (which are also new arrivals), are referred to as "forms to hang paint on." But that is nothing so remarkably new, thinking of the robes and hearts. Often the image has been used as a constant, repetitively, to permit the painting to move as freely in its experience as impulse and recognitions might permit. Insofar as the phrase refers to gates and trees, that sense of "to hang paint on" is inevitably interesting. One is sure it was no casually determined expression.

The Crommelynck Gate can be found at 172 rue de Grenelle, Paris, the address of Aldo Crommelynck, master engraver and printer, who with his brother has collaborated in a singular range of etchings, from those of Picasso and Matisse to Jasper Johns and Dine himself, with whom he has worked on several projects in recent years. This gate is the entrance to the atelier and residence. The place has a grand and imposing air, somewhat like a hospital or official residence. Dine must have passed through this particular gate many times, to sit at an immaculate work bench, attended by very specific provision and respect, to *make art*, as is said. So these gates (or gate) have an unexpected parallel to those gates most common in American habit, possibly those of a factory. The other gates one thinks of quickly are the cemetery's (or heaven's):

Whatever might prove the case, the fact that this image has a literal source is useful. One supposes that most of Dine's images are so founded, but again the accessible fact of this one gives means to recognize the particular modes of investment and change he works with. It is interesting that the image is intently centered, that one sees that much of it which would be commonly seen walking toward it from some short distance away. One is reminded of a cinematic device or focus, curiously, as though one were the 'eye' of a camera.

In quite another sense, a poem of Thomas Hardy's recounts the awesome terror of approaching such a gate—the gate to death itself—to see on its other side the ghoulish objects of despair and terminus beckoning. Then he asks, were it simpler to pass through and have done, rather than to live on knowing one will one day come again? These images depend an almost elegant insistence of tracery upon a vast emptiness of opened space. The formal fascinates because it is all that is there to hold any concept, any possibility, of place. But there is nothing seemingly behind it, but *Fog,* but blackness. Even at home (*Vermont*) it remains ambiguously inviting.

Is one to stop here? All art would wish to remain at one with its human limit, to be so contained. Clearly there is to be an end. But here one cannot know whether this is its sign, or simply the thing *we* see, waiting. RC

The Crommelynck Gate,
172 rue de Grenelle, Paris
Photograph: Nancy Dine

The Crommelynck Gate 1981
acrylic and charcoal on canvas
with wooden strip
96 x 169¼ (2 panels)
Collection Mr. and Mrs. Samuel
A. Lindenbaum

The Crommelynck Gate series began in 1981,
a year after the Trees. They were inspired by
the gate outside the house and studio of Aldo
Crommelynck, the great French printer with
whom I've worked since 1973. For eight years
I could see the gate from the table where I made
etchings, and it became a symbol for me of
France and my friendship with Aldo and his
wife, Pep. I saw in its arabesque shapes a way
to make a painting that would be the closest I
would ever come to abstraction. Of course, it
didn't end up that way. It never does.

I wanted to celebrate my friendship with
him and his closeness to my family. His
relationship to my children has been more than
avuncular. At the same time I wanted to deal
purely with paint and I thought the gate was a
neutral enough subject for that. Its beautiful,
curvilinear shapes relate to older art, an idea I
responded to. Sometimes, though, it looks like
an old brass bedstead. After painting it, the real
gate now looks very small.

The Crommelynck Gate
(The Quilt) 1981
shellac, charcoal, oil, acrylic and
pastel on linen and paper
69 x 86¾

Fragment of the Crommelynck
Gate 1981
acrylic on paper
60 x 40

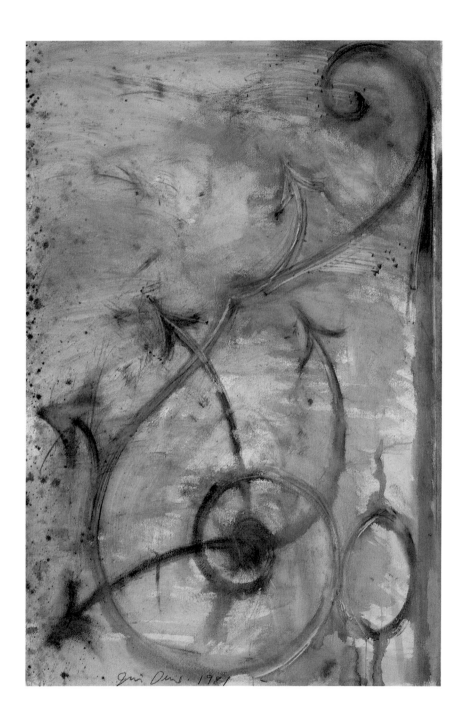

*Study for the Sculpture of The Crommelynck Gate
with Tools (Black Shoe)*
*Study for the Sculpture of The Crommelynck Gate
with Tools (St. Leonards)*

*Study for the Sculpture of The
Crommelynck Gate with Tools
(Black Shoe)*   1983
charcoal, enamel and pastel on
paper with objects
70½ x 89
Courtesy The Pace Gallery

These drawing-collages are part of a group of
five done in London in the spring of 1983 (see
p 6, *St. Leonards*). I had nowhere to make the
large studies for *The Crommelynck Gate with
Tools,* which will have tools welded to the gate.
A friend offered me the perfect environment—
her empty house which was about to be gutted
and remodeled. The place was a wreck but I
found some things left by the previous owner.
I practiced moving these objects onto the gates
where they might be most effective. Even
though the pictures are large they are still very
much drawings.

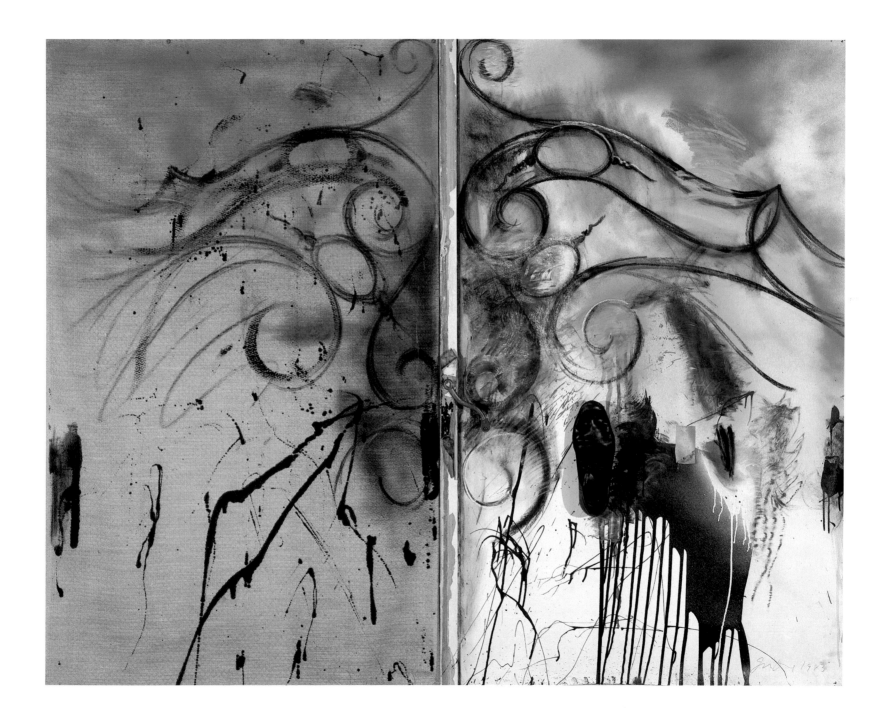

The artist with
The Crommelynck Gate with Tools, Los Angeles, 1983.
Photographs: Nancy Dine

The Crommelynck Gate with Tools 1983
bronze
108 x 132 x 36

This sculpture will be cast in an edition of three bronzes. It's twice as big as the actual gate in Paris, and not faithful in replicating all its details. There are tree branches on each side (as in *The Fence* painting), that will also be cast in bronze. I've taken direct wax castings of tools and then heated and twisted them to change the shapes. They will also be cast in bronze and welded onto the gate frame to stick out, front and back. Then the whole piece will be painted.

These gates are a symbol of my great ambition for my art, particularly in their scale.

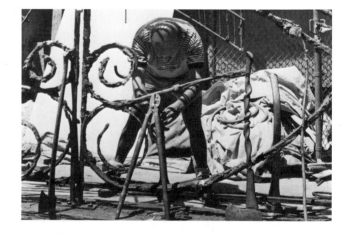

142

For J. D.

Pass on by, love,
wait by that garden gate.
Swing on, up
on heaven's gate.

The confounding, confronted
pictures of world
brought to signs
of its persistent self

are here in all colors, sizes—
and hearts as big as all outdoors,
a weather of spaces,
intervals between silences.

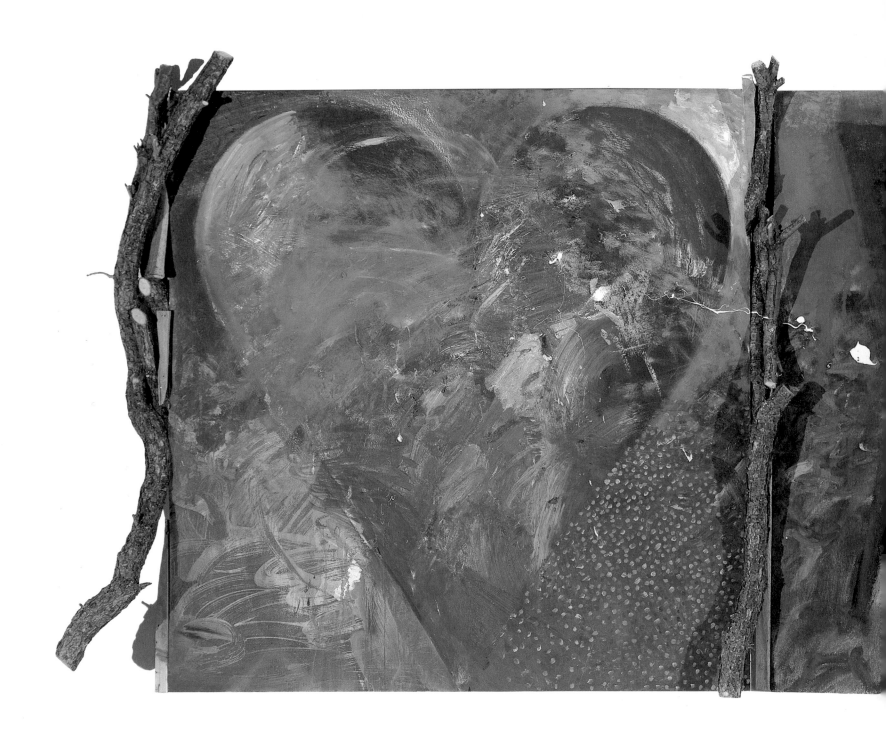

The Death at South Kensington,
2nd Version (Piñon)   1983
oil on masonite with objects
52 x 210 (4 panels)
Courtesy The Pace Gallery

Biography

1935–46
Born in Cincinnati, Ohio on 16 June 1935.
Children's classes at the Cincinnati Art Museum.

1947
Mother died; went to live with maternal grandparents.

1951–53
Attended adult night classes at the Cincinnati Art Academy
while in high school.

1954–58
BFA, June 1957, Ohio University, Athens. One year of
post-graduate work studying drawing with Frederick Leach.

1957
Married Nancy Minto.

1958–59
Moved to New York City; taught at the Rhodes School.
Founded Judson Gallery with Claes Oldenburg and Marc
Ratliff. First performance of *The Smiling Workman* made there
in 1959. Joined the Reuben Gallery with Allan Kaprow, Lucas
Samaras, George Segal and Robert Whitman.

1960
Performed *Car Crash* at the Reuben Gallery.

1961
Joined Martha Jackson Gallery; gallery subsidy permitted
full-time painting. Had first one-man show of Ties and other
objects in the winter of 1961–62.

1962
Met Ileana Sonnabend who bought paintings of tools with real
objects to show at her newly opened Paris gallery; the
beginning of a fourteen-year association with the Sonnabend
Gallery. Began psychoanalysis.

1963
Found photograph of original "bathrobe" in *The New York
Times Magazine* and made first paintings of it as a "self-
portrait."

1964
Showed at the Venice Bienn

1965
Made first cast-aluminum s
Night's Dream for Actor's W
of Heart image.

1966
Visited London for the first

1967
Moved to London with fami
by friendship with so-called

1969
Visited Paris for the first tim
Sonnabend Gallery, Paris.

1970
Retrospective at the Whitne
New York.

1971–74
Moved from London to Ver
in Paris with Aldo Crommely
Sonnabend Gallery, New Yo

1975
Began to draw from the figur
for six years.

1976
Joined The Pace Gallery, New
large figure drawings in the w

1980
Began large paintings of single
part of each year in London.

1981
Began first painting of the Cro

150

1982

Wintered in Los Angeles making 76-foot-long paintings for Gene Summers, an old friend. Early summer exhibition of Hearts, Gates and Trees at Waddington Gallery, London. Late summer in Copenhagen making eighteen-panel picture titled *Lessons in Nuclear Peace* for new library in the Louisiana Museum. Began bronze casting of sculpture in London.

1983

Wintered in Los Angeles casting *The Crommelynck Gate with Tools* in bronze at Otis Parsons Art School. Began series of paintings called *The Death at South Kensington* in memory of the botanical artist Rory McEwen. Spent the summer in Aspen, Colorado; continued painting and casting bronze with Mark Anderson in Walla Walla, Washington. Autumn exhibition of completed Crommelynck Gate and related works at the Los Angeles County Museum of Art. Exhibition of twenty-five etchings of wife Nancy at Chicago Art Institute, October.

1984

Continues painting and sculpture of Gates and other themes in London and Vermont. Retrospective exhibition of five themes organized for February opening at the Walker Art Center.

Selected Bibliography

For a thorough bibliography prior to 1980, see: Shapiro, David. *Jim Dine*. New York: Harry N. Abrams, Inc., 1981.

Catalogues

Chicago, Richard Gray Gallery. *Jim Dine, An Exhibition of Recent Figure Drawings, 1978 – 1980*, text by David Shapiro, 1981.

Articles

Ackley, Clifford S. "Face in a Frame," *Art News,* September 1982, pp 63 – 64.

Artner, Alan G. "All I am Here For is to Paint and Draw," *Chicago Tribune,* 20 February 1983, Section 6, p 19.

Ashberry, John. "Metaphysical Overtones," *New York,* 11 February 1980, pp 72 – 73.

Field, Richard S. "On Recent Woodcuts," *The Print Collector's Newsletter,* March – April 1982, pp 1 – 6.

Gardner, Paul. "Will Success Spoil Bob & Jim, Louise & Larry?," *Art News,* November 1982, pp 102 – 109.

Glenn, Constance W. "Artist's Dialogue: A Conversation with Jim Dine," *Architectural Digest,* November 1982, pp 74 – 82.

Henry, Gerrit. "New York Reviews," *Art News,* March 1982, p 210.

Kramer, Hilton. "Art: Jim Dine Revisits Heart Motif with Tools," *The New York Times,* 20 November 1981, p C26.

Liebmann, Lisa. "New York Reviews," *Artforum,* February 1982, pp 87 – 88.

Schwartz, Ellen. "New York Reviews," *Art News,* April 1980, pp 183 – 184.

Acknowledgments

Without the wholehearted support of Jim Dine, this exhibition could not have been realized. His insightful commentaries on specific works are an invaluable contribution to the catalogue. The idea for this exhibition came from Graham W. J. Beal, Keeper of the Sainsbury Centre for the Visual Arts, University of East Anglia, Norwich, England, who, in his former capacity as Chief Curator of the Walker Art Center, began work on it. He made the initial selection of paintings and wrote the essay on Dine's five themes after extensive discussions with the artist.

Nancy Dine, the artist's wife, provided valuable assistance with many aspects of the exhibition's preparation. Arnold Glimcher, Director of The Pace Gallery, New York, was helpful throughout all phases of the exhibition's preparation and Judith Harney, also of The Pace Gallery, helped us locate important examples of Dine's work in public and private collections. Information regarding many works in Dine's possession was provided by Blake Summers, the artist's assistant. Louise Bernbaum, an American who lives in England, was enormously helpful as editor of the Beal and Dine texts.

Particular thanks are due the many individuals and institutional lenders who permitted their works by Jim Dine to be shown in this exhibition. To be deprived of those for the length of the exhibition's national tour is no small sacrifice, and their sympathetic response to Walker Art Center's request for loans made this exhibition possible. On behalf of Jim and the Walker Art Center, I acknowledge the generosity of these individuals and institutions.

Many Walker Art Center staff members were involved in preparing this exhibition and it is a pleasure to acknowledge their contributions.

Martin Friedman, Director

Lenders to the Exhibition

Akron Art Museum, Akron, Ohio
Allen Memorial Art Museum, Oberlin College, Ohio
Mr. and Mrs. Harry W. Anderson
The Art Museum, Princeton University, Princeton,
New Jersey
Mr. and Mrs. E. A. Bergman
Mr. and Mrs. Fred Carr
Byron and Eileen Cohen
Douglas S. Cramer
Mrs. Julius E. Davis
Jim Dine
Mr. and Mrs. Asher B. Edelman
Joel and Anne Ehrenkranz
Milly and Arnold Glimcher
Graham Gund
Hirshhorn Museum and Sculpture Garden, Smithsonian
Institution, Washington, D. C.
Paul and Camille Oliver Hoffmann
Mr. and Mrs. Sidney Kahn
Mr. and Mrs. Aron B. Katz
Sydney and Frances Lewis
Mr. and Mrs. Samuel H. Lindenbaum
Museum of Fine Arts, Boston, Massachusetts
The Museum of Modern Art, New York, New York
Mr. and Mrs. Morton G. Neumann
Newport Harbor Art Museum, Newport Beach, California
Nancy M. O'Boyle
Pace Editions Inc., New York, New York
The Pace Gallery, New York, New York
Philadelphia Museum of Art, Philadelphia, Pennsylvania
Stuart and Anne Robinowitz
Eileen Rosenau
Sonnabend Gallery, New York, New York
Gene R. Summers
The Washington Art Consortium: Cheney Cowles Memorial
State Museum, Spokane; Museum of Art, Washington State
University, Pullman; Tacoma Art Museum, Tacoma; the
Henry Gallery, University of Washington, Seattle; the Western
Gallery, Western Washington State University, Bellingham;
the Whatcom Museum of History and Art, Bellingham,
Washington
Whitney Museum of American Art, New York, New York
One Private Collection

Reproduction Credits

Courtesy Abbeville Press: pp 16 (right), 23, 24, 37, 83, 131,
139
Courtesy Harry N. Abrams, Inc.: pp 53, 65, 97, 98, 99, 103
Courtesy Akron Art Museum: p 92
Courtesy Allen Memorial Art Museum, Oberlin College:
p 75
Courtesy The Art Museum, Princeton University: p 57
Courtesy Mr. and Mrs. E. A. Bergman: p 69 (bottom)
Courtesy Leo Castelli Gallery: p 20
Geoffrey Clements, courtesy Estate of Myron Orlofsky: p 21
Courtesy Douglas S. Cramer: p 110
Courtesy The Larry Gagosian Gallery: p 29
Courtesy Hirshhorn Museum and Sculpture Garden,
Smithsonian Institution: p 27
Courtesy Sydney and Frances Lewis: p 81
Dennis McWaters, courtesy Sydney and Frances Lewis: p 73
Lou Marcus, courtesy Mr. and Mrs. Aron B. Katz: p 123
Courtesy Musée National d'Art Moderne, Centre Georges
Pompidou: p 38 (bottom)
Courtesy Museum of Fine Arts, Boston: p 129
Courtesy The Museum of Modern Art, New York: pp 13,
38 (top), 60, 61, 62, 63
Courtesy Newport Harbor Art Museum: p 30
Courtesy Nancy M. O'Boyle: p 69 (top)
Courtesy The Pace Gallery: cover, pp 2, 6, 10, 33, 34, 40, 41,
42, 45, 82, 87, 91, 105, 109, 111, 113, 115, 117, 121, 124, 125,
127, 128, 137, 141, 146
Courtesy Philadelphia Museum of Art: p 85
Lawrence Reynolds, courtesy Los Angeles County Museum
of Art: p 143
Lawrence Reynolds, courtesy Gene R. Summers: p 54
E. G. Schempf, courtesy Byron and Eileen Cohen: p 101
Courtesy St. Louis Art Museum: p 17
Courtesy Sonnabend Gallery: p 51
Courtesy Gene R. Summers: p 78
Walker Art Center, courtesy Mrs. Julius E. Davis: p 26, 67
Courtesy Walker Art Center: p 132, 133, 138
Courtesy The Washington Art Consortium: p 55
David Wharton, courtesy Dallas Museum of Fine Arts: p 31
Courtesy Whitney Museum of American Art: p 15
Courtesy Yale University Art Gallery: p 16 (left), 76

Travel Schedule

19 February–15 April 1984
Walker Art Center

13 May–24 June 1984
Phoenix Art Museum

22 July–3 September 1984
St. Louis Art Museum

22 September–11 November 1984
Akron Art Museum

7 December 1984–20 January 1985
Albright-Knox Art Gallery, Buffalo

20 February–28 April 1985
Hirshhorn Museum and Sculpture Garden,
Washington, D. C.

155

Index of Illustrations

Afternoon Robe 33
Art of Painting No. 2, The 57 – 58
Axe 69
Balcony 85
Big Black Work Wall 50
Black Crommelynck Gate, The 45
Black Garden Tools 21
Black Shovel, The 51
Blue (painting) 125
Blue (print) 133
Blue Clamp 109
Blue of Autumn with a Red Light, The 128
Brace and Bit (from *Untitled Tool Series*) 63
C Clamp (from *Untitled Tool Series*) 63
Cardinal 81
Charcoal Self-Portrait in a Cement Garden 75
Coming in the Sun 101
Crommelynck Gate, The 137
Crommelynck Gate (The Quilt), The 138
Crommelynck Gate with Tools, The 143
Death at South Kensington (October), The 115
Death at South Kensington, 2nd Version (Piñon), The 146 – 148
Desire (The Charterhouse) 87 – 88
Double Green Diptych 131
Double Isometric Self-Portrait (Serape) 15
Dry-Wall Hammer (from *Untitled Tool Series*) 61

Five Feet of Colorful Tools 13
5-Bladed Saw (from *Untitled Tool Series*) 60
Flesh Bathroom with Yellow Light and Objects 17
Fool's House (Jasper Johns) 20
Four Hearts of Sidney Close 117
Four Robes Existing in This Vale of Tears 78 – 79
Fragment of the Crommelynck Gate 139
French Letter, The 24
German Blackness, A 110
Hammer Doorway, The 54
Hoof Nipper (from *Untitled Tool Series*) 62
I'm Painting with My Animals 99
In Advance of the Broken Arm (Marcel Duchamp) 16
Japanese Paper Company, The 41
Jerusalem Nights 91
Lawnmower 16
Light Comes upon the Old City 82
L'Oeil Cacodylate (Francis Picabia) 38
Nancy and I at Ithaca (Straw Heart) 37
Night Forces Painterliness to Show Itself in a Clearer Way, The 34
Object (Meret Oppenheim) 38
Oil Can (from *Untitled Tool Series*) 62
Our Life Here 23
Painting a Fortress for the Heart 40
Painting Around Mount Zion 92 – 93
Painting (Cruising) (La Chasse) 105 – 106
Palette (Self-Portrait No. 1) 30
Pliers (from *Untitled Tool Series*) 61
Poulenc 103
Red Robe with Hatchet (Self-Portrait) 73
Red Robe #2 76
Red Tree, Flesh Tree, A Carnival Tree: The Painting 42
Richly Grown Drawing, A 132
Romancing in Late Winter 111
Rose and Grey 127

Self-Portrait Next to a Colored Window 31
Shears 26
Shovel 69
Small Shower 53
Study for the Sculpture of The Crommelynck Gate with Tools (Black Shoe) 141
Study for the Sculpture of The Crommelynck Gate with Tools (St. Leonards) 6
Swaying in the Florida Night 133
3 Palettes (3 Self-Portrait Studies) 29
Tiger Lies at the Bottom of Our Garden, A 124
Tonight There is Weather 83
Tree (The Kimono) 129
Tree in the Shadow of Our Intimacy, A 123
Two Mighty Robes at Night in Jerusalem, frontispiece
Untitled (Gloves) 97
Untitled 1973 (Monument) 55
Untitled 1974 (pitchfork) 67
Untitled (Red Clippers) 27
Untitled 1974 (saw) 65
Untitled (Tricky Teeth) 98
View in Sologne (for Pep and Aldo), A 121
Wall and the Fence, The 113
Work Horse, The 10

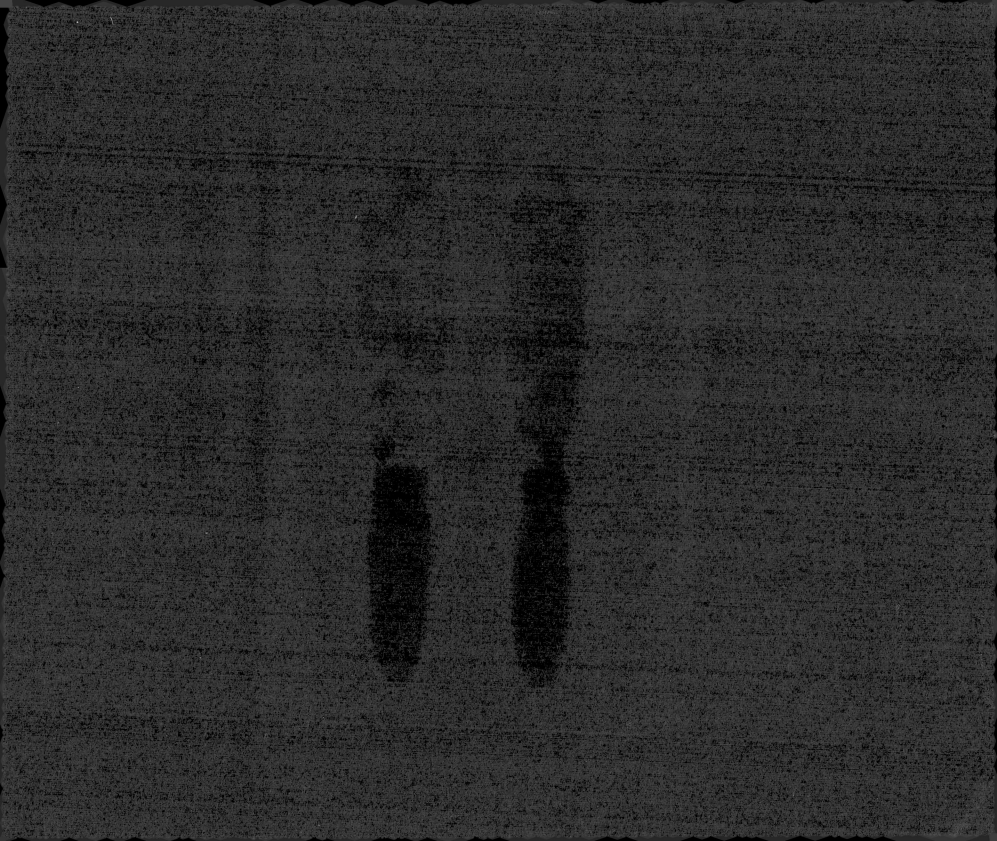